BEGINNING JEWELRY

BEGINNING JEWELRY

James F. Warwick

CHARLES SCRIBNER'S SONS · NEW YORK

In memory of my brother Bill

Library of Congress Cataloging in Publication Data
Warwick, James F.
  Beginning jewelry.
  1. Jewelry making—Amateurs' manuals.
I. Title.
TT212.W37   739.27'4   79-836
ISBN 0-684-16143-5

1 3 5 7 9 11 13 15 17 19 M/P 20 18 16 14 12 10 8 6 4 2

Printed in the United States of America

Design by James F. Warwick

Acknowledgments

To Dick Kyle firstly. Without his photographic skill and his willingness to "do it over, to be sure" this book might never have come into being. It surely would not have had the graphic impact I feel it has now. Any photographic faults it may have reflect my insistence on doing it my way.

To four current colleagues and close friends: Clarence Bunch, John Lidstone, Shirley Kramer, and Olga Young, whose initial encouragement and continued support is deeply appreciated.

To Dudley Shannon, president of Allcraft Tool and Supply Company, for kindly letting me borrow whatever I wanted—for as long as I needed it. To Joe Scala, his right-hand man, for gathering and organizing these items, and also for some very sage advice on how to photograph them. And to those folks in the back shop for taking the time to talk, point out, ask, and express interest in the production of this book.

To Lillian Telegadas, who typed and retyped, and retyped again, various stages of the copy. She accepted with warm good grace the return of her pristine typewritten work covered with scrawls and corrections to be yet retyped.

To those people at Scribners, a marvelously professional and supportive group, who have been assistance personified.

To those former classmates, colleagues, and the host of professional and personal friends who have taught me so much—and not merely about the craft of jewelry: John Leary, Jack Arends, Bill Mahoney, Justin Schorr, Mildred Fairchild, Edwin Ziegfeld, Marvin (Red) Garner, Bill Gambling, Ben Goldsmith, Lee Hall, Frank D'Amato, George Horn, John Ames, Ed Welling, and Milton Hellerbach.

And neither least nor last, to the legions of students who by their questions and spirit also teach. I am indebted to them for what I have learned.

Contents

INTRODUCTION: JEWELRY AS A CREATIVE EXPRESSION

The beginnings of jewelry as body ornament probably lie with the beginnings of man himself. From the time Homo sapiens discovered the attractions of a bone, a twig, or a feather stuck in his hair, body ornament has been as much a personal and social part of man as clothing and shelter. At no time in recorded history has man failed to employ some form, however minor, of personal adornment. These have ranged from a tiny dark-colored ribbon on a hatband in Puritan society to the grandiose headdresses, earrings, belt buckles, breastplates, pendants, bracelets, and crowns of religious god-king figures. Body ornament, and then specific jewelry items, were used as symbols of achievement, emblems of association, signs of wealth or religious affiliation, or purely and simply to enhance the wearer as well as for personal pleasure. Interestingly enough, body ornament has almost never been a casual gesture, or of only passing or temporary interest. The nomadic tribesman content with living in a hut of skins or mud, thrown together in a few hours, nonetheless spent weeks and months fashioning his personal jewelry.

Among those qualities which make man unique on this earth are his ability and readiness to devise and use tools. This trait found pragmatic expression in the creation of traps, knives, spears, and shovels, which in turn were used to help him construct jewelry. Man began to bend and beat, heat and hammer, and drill and dome with his tools on stone, shell, wood, and especially metal. It was with his discovery of metal, particularly precious metals with their wondrous properties of ductility, strength, and polish, that man's expressive nature flowered. More than any other single development in the cloudy early history of jewelry, it was the discovery and use of gold and silver that focused his attention toward beauty as an end in itself.

Well over a thousand years B.C. most of the basic metal-working processes used today were being exercised in the construction of jewelry items. Evidences exist of metal being beaten, chased, formed, soldered, and filigreed. And with these developments jewelry became a conscious integral facet of society, a reflection of the emotional and intellectual regard in which craftsmen held their society. Jewelry conformed to beliefs widely held, and it has also stood removed and opposed. When ostentation was frowned upon, jewelry production and elaborate craft work decreased; when society altered its tenor and sought expression, jewelry also experienced a rebirth. At a time during the industrial revolution when the machine began to alter man's work patterns radically, many craftsmen refused to acknowledge, much less respond to, these changes in technology and times. They continued their solitary productions—to the demise of *meaningful* craft work. At another and more recent time, torn by strife and conflict, the craftsman has been able to operate on two levels. On one he has been in the forefront of protest, and on the other his work has found reflective expression in a serene and peaceful manifestation of beauty.

In our contemporary and often sterile environment an attraction to hand-crafted work—production as well as acquisition—is growing. The psychological need to feel as one with an item is very strong. There is an almost conscious satisfaction derived from

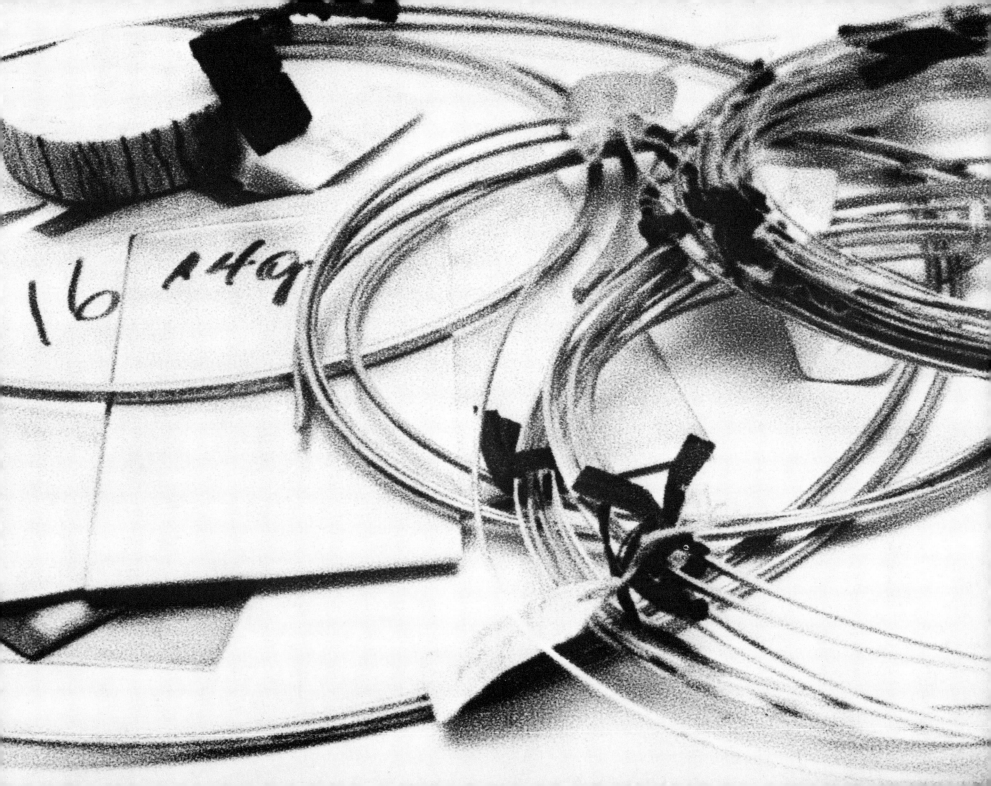

knowing that a crafted piece is the result of another human being's concept, concern, and constructive abilities. But as strong as the purchaser's feeling unquestionably is, an even deeper satisfaction is gained as a craft producer. Witness the enormous increase in the past few years in craft offerings as serious college-credit courses, or as casual private and personal teaching/learning activities. Indeed, one large American university (Boston University) has begun a major organizational division devoted exclusively to craft work. Other universities are following suit, and these are not just expanded craft offerings within the structure of a typical college art department. Too many universities and colleges are still sadly under the sway of the "fine arts" faculty, who refuse to acknowledge that "craft" exists. It is even more ironic that the craft work being produced around them is frequently superior to their own work. Also reflecting the growing national interest in crafts is the tremendous increase in the sale of crafts and craft supplies.

The American public is discovering what craftsmen have known for a long time: Making a craft is very, very satisfying and very, very pleasurable. And, in this writer's opinion, jewelry is the most satisfying and pleasurable craft of them all. Its basics are easy to learn, and yet capable of being extended to enormously complex dimensions. The end product, of course, speaks for itself. Besides having an inherent appeal, the jewelry item is usually valuable—often very valuable. It can be worn. It relates to both wearer and maker very intimately. When worn it shows itself, becoming in effect a moving display.

The time spent making an item of jewelry can be counted in minutes—or it may take literally days and weeks. And even as an item can be assembled over a short time, production time may have to be extended over weeks or months—or indefinitely. The construction of a piece of jewelry may be worked in with the construction of other pieces, or worked on very much by itself. The materials and tools involved do not go bad, do not dry out, do not get unworkably stiff while waiting, do not change color. Things left remain just as they are without cover, container, cap, or seal.

Making jewelry doesn't require large bowls, screens, vats, presses, fans, crocks, or work tables. It does not obligate the craftsman to wear special clothing, gloves, or masks (although it must be noted that many jewelers wear a face mask when polishing). The basic material doesn't have a tendency to spill, overrun, boil over, pour, or drip. And nothing involved in the production entails much time spent wiping, washing up, cleaning, storing, or capping. The preparations for working don't require any "gearing up," soaking, mixing (excepting simple pours of simple fluids and compounds), or stirring. Getting ready to work on jewelry is no more involved than sitting down, reaching for the appropriate tool, perhaps lighting a torch if needed, or pouring some flux —if necessary. Stopping is just as direct and simple: Shut off the torch, if lit, and pour back the flux, if you want to save it.

The equipment employed is comparatively tiny, and it is tidy. With the exception of a flexible shaft unit and a large (but not huge) B tank torch unit, all of the author's own equipment and tools fit easily into a converted artist's paint box. The work area needed, and used by the author, measures less than 2 by 3 feet, and with a couple of shelves off to one side for solutions and compounds, everything needed can fit within this area and is within arm's length.

Not lastly, one of the very real attractions to the jewelry craft is its unique blending of technical skill, design sensitivity, and intellectual perception. No matter how often one solders, or how often a piece is cut or beaten, the pleasure and thrill remain, for each time it seems like a new activity. It is an exciting craft.

This book grew out of my experiences working with students just beginning in jewelry. They ranged from youngsters in their teens, recently out of high school, to retired senior citizens taking classes for purely personal pleasure and interest. A few of these students had experience with tools, but most did not. Some had backgrounds in art, but many did not.

The underlying assumption in what follows is that the beginning jeweler has no experience with tools, and perhaps even only limited conceptual understanding of their use. Consequently, some of the in-

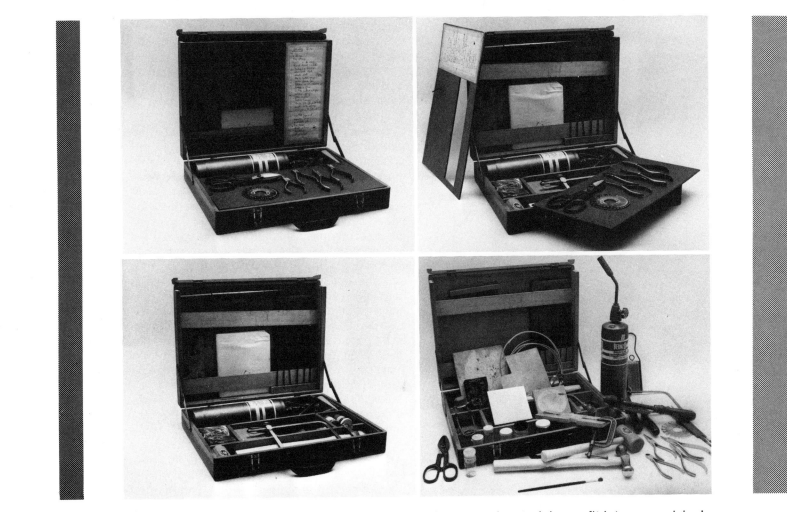

As the above four views suggest, all of the basic equipment and materials can fit into a surprisingly small area. Here an old paint box has been converted to accommodate all the equipment.

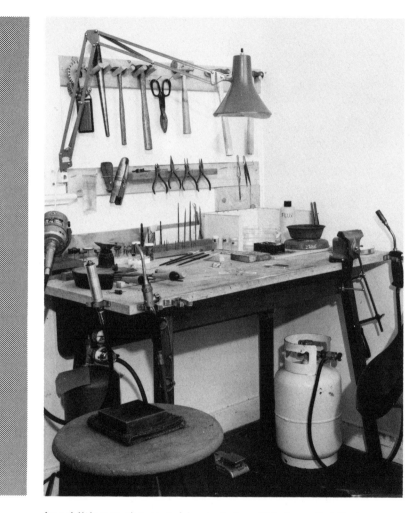

In addition to the portable workshop this is a slightly larger, but not much more luxurious, working area. It is literally a table in a corner of a spare bedroom.

formation, and many of the illustrations, may appear elementary to readers who have a working knowledge of tools. However, those who feel they do know or at least have an acquaintance with tools are cautioned: The equipment employed by the jeweler, while it may resemble other common tools, is not the same. A light tap on a nail with a polished forming hammer would undoubtedly drive the nail, but just as surely destroy the face of the hammer. In brief, the book is designed for the beginner who doesn't know a thing about tools, their use, or their care and conditioning.

It was apparent as semesters and then years passed that certain ways of teaching, or rather, impressing, a technique or an approach seemed to be more successful than others. From this realization developed what has been referred to jocularly by students as the "fact sheets." These were simply single pages of fundamental information for each of the basic techniques. This information spelled out in outline format, in direct and clear terms, the why, the how, the when and ways with tools, techniques, and the use of the basic materials. Additions and deletions were made as students gained experience and evaluated the fact sheets. Here again it was discovered that certain concepts were established by having them repeated in a catchy fashion. It was also discovered that certain basics were imparted more successfully by illustrating them with exaggeratedly large drawings.

Beginning Jewelry, very much like those sheets, operates on a direct and simple premise: to discuss and show in sufficient detail that which is necessary for you to know to begin making jewelry without personal instruction. The book also contains information and illustrations which the author feels are interesting and helpful in support of this learning process.

The book does not go very far afield or cover that which could be considered tangential to making jewelry. Power shears for cutting metal, or large rolling mills, or draw plates for wire (for thinning it) may be viewed as essential by some craftsmen. This craftsman is not among them. Nor does the book address certain advanced techniques such as electroplating or granulation. To the experienced craftsman this and other decisions may be viewed as glaring errors of omission. Apologies are offered to them and to you too if you have been convinced that a jewelry book must have certain techniques, tools, and a host of related information shown in specific ways.

This book is also a reflection of the experiences many of my students have had with other jewelry books. The problems many found in trying to work with these books stemmed from their being either absurdly simple or incomprehensibly complex. A book that details which end of a hammer is the head and which is the handle is not much better than another detailing how to electroplate while ignoring why and how to anneal.

Another comment with regard to jewelry craft books. Most beginners find themselves perplexed by the scale of tools and equipment. Scale itself is not important, but when used as a guide and the beginner is left to believe it is important, it becomes very important. It is difficult to comprehend quickly that the saw blade held in the hand, if blown up, would resemble a six-foot-long cross-cut saw used to fell mighty oaks. The beginner is asked to judge the blade size necessary by holding this blade next to the edge of a piece of silver thinner than a dime! I do not know any serious craftsman or sensible student who does his measuring this way.

Another objection students have raised with jewelry-technique books—and I agree—is the rigid "Do it this way only" approach so many take. If you can cut metal upside down and backward, while standing on your head—fine, do so. The point is, really, to cut the metal. Certainly try the method suggested, for it usually makes sense, but it also may not be the only way of undertaking a technique. This book's section "Basic Techniques," for example, is presented in the order in which one usually begins and then proceeds to make a piece. But this order is not absolute, nor are the specifics within those techniques presented.

There is no reason why you cannot drill before you cut; or bend, then cut; or polish before you bend. Do not be afraid of experimenting. Don't break tools in the process, but find out what the metal will do. Much of the pleasure in making jewelry is devising your own methods and unique ways of doing a job.

One of the ways you may lessen any early anxiety over "destroying" a piece of silver is to set out quite deliberately to, in fact, destroy a piece. Cut snips out of it, bend it until it breaks, beat the metal with nails and punches, rub it on sandpaper and on the sidewalk. Hammer the metal until it fractures. In brief, see what abuse the material will take. A number of discoveries should result. You will be surprised at how malleable it is, how easy it is to scratch and mar. Yet, just as surprising is the metal's strength. It is a durable material and does not come apart easily.

No direct effort was made to cover jewelry design in this volume. It is to be the focus of the forthcoming companion book. Nonetheless, the author's work is shown for illustrative purposes in process and finished. Hopefully these examples suggest the author's strong interest and concern with good design.

A good design executed adequately is to be preferred over a poor design executed superbly. A drawing pad should go hand in hand with this book. Sketch your ideas, draw jewelry designs, detail parts, make construction notes. The book need not be shown to anyone, and probably should not be. Don't be afraid to try an idea in a drawing. The jewelry item developed out of thin air, without time spent on drawing and planning, is almost guaranteed to result in a bad bauble. Good design in jewelry does not just happen. It needs time, effort, and no little work. Provide every opportunity for yourself and the exercise of free-flowing ideas.

Learning any craft takes time and patience. Your confidence will build with your willingness to conceive, plan, and produce. A valuable artifact is not only satisfying in itself but serves as a strong stimulus for still more time spent in developing technical skills and design sensitivity.

BASIC MATERIALS

silver and other materials

The material most widely used by jewelry craftsmen is sterling silver. The term "sterling" means simply that copper has been added in a proportion of 75 parts to 925 parts of silver. With this proportion, and only with this proportion, may the resulting alloy be referred to legally as "sterling" silver. Incidentally, the craftsman has the same obligation in pronouncing his crafted item as "sterling" only if it is, in fact, *all* sterling silver. This means the piece has all of its parts—pins, hooks, fastenings, and so on—in sterling.

The reason for adding copper to pure silver is to give the base metal added strength. Silver in its purest state is much too soft for typical use, too soft to form into durable shapes, and almost too soft to work with. When pure silver is used it is almost invariably limited to gallery wire, which is used to form holdings (bezels) for stones, wood, or ivory. Pure silver in use this way is easily shaped to fit a stone and will then, when braced, hold its form. All reference to metal that follows, unless clearly indicated otherwise, is to sterling silver.

Silver, along with gold and platinum, is considered one of the three precious metals. It is in its own right a conspiculously unusual substance. It is incredibly malleable, yet surprisingly strong. An ounce of silver may be drawn (stretched) into a wire well over three miles long without breaking. The metal may be thinned to a fineness of less than one-hundred-thousandth of an inch. It is a superb conductor of heat, electricity, and light. Indeed, it conducts electricity so well that it is the principal material used to effect contacts in switches, computers, and assorted conductors and circuits. It is the material most suitable for photographic film—because it greatly intensifies light striking a sensitized surface. Without silver, it is fair to say, the photographic industry could not exist. It can be incised, etched, scratched,

beaten, bent, carved, cast, deliberately oxidized (blackened), or polished to a mirror gloss. Add to these factors silver's inherent ability to withstand rust and its value to industry becomes readily apparent. It is a truly remarkable material, which the sensitive craftsman comes to appreciate and respect the more he works with it and comes to know it.

The weight of silver is measured by the troy ounce —which is 14.6 ounces of one avoirdupois pound. Craftsmen refer to and order sterling silver more often, however, by gauge (thickness), by general configuration (sheet, wire, shape—that is, square, round, half round, and so on), and by size in inches (length and width for sheet, or in length only for wire). With the exception of casting granules, it is rarely purchased by weight alone.

The most important measure for craftsmen is the gauge of the metal. This is a simple measurable standard that may be determined with a circular metal disk marked for gauge. The most common are Brown & Sharpe and American Standard, available at craft-supply stores, and operated by fitting the metal to be measured into slots on the outside of a metal disk. Note that both sheet and wire are measured this way—not by or through the hole. The thicker the metal, the lower the gauge number. Silver can be ordered from suppliers in any gauge desired, but most craft-supply houses stock only "popular" gauges and the most convenient of these tend to be even numbers: 8, 10, 12, 14, 16, 18, 20, 22, and 24 gauges.

And of course, other measuring devices are used: a ring gauge, which is simply a series of rings graduated in size that correspond to established sizes of ring measures; and a ring mandrel, which is a tapered steel shaft—that may also be graduated in sizes, corresponding to the ring measure.

A typical order by a craftsman might then read as

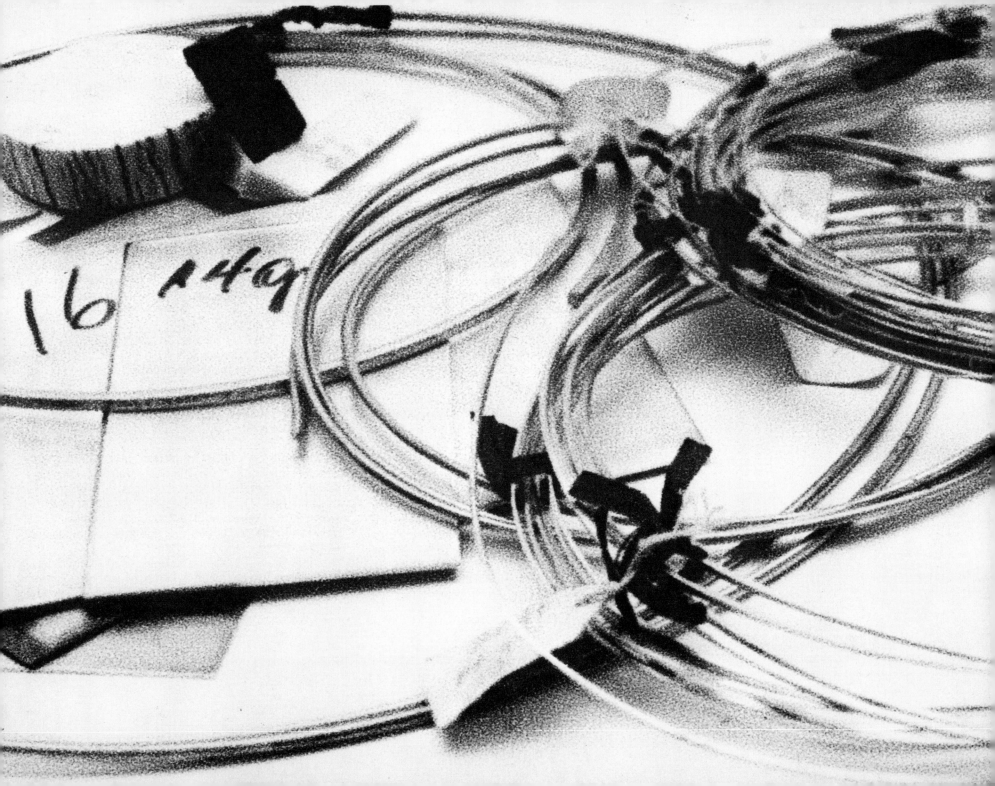

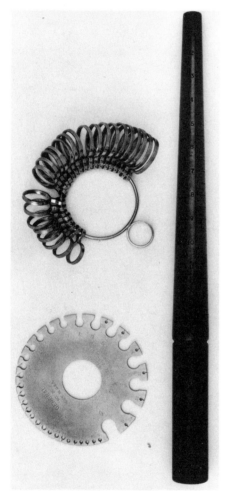

Along with the B&S gauge, other "measuring" tools include the ring "sizer" (or gauge) and in conjunction with it the ring mandrel. The ring mandrel can be purchased with graduations that correspond to the ring sizer.

follows: *one piece of 18-gauge, 4-by-6-inch sheet sterling.* And an order for wire might read: *one foot of 14-gauge square sterling wire.* The weight (and therefore the cost) for each of these can be calculated from detailed weight charts available at most craft-supply houses. Sample charts are shown on page 15 for easy comparison. The above order for sheet silver measuring 4 by 6 inches in 18 gauge, for example, weighs 5.30 ounces. The cost then is arrived at by calculating 5.30 times (current cost). At this writing, it is around $6.66 per ounce. (It has gone as high as $8.25, and fluctuates.) That makes the sheet cost $35.30. The 14-gauge square wire weighs .269 ounces per inch—so .269 times 24 inches = 6.45 ounces times $6.66 = $42.96.

The point, of course, is to check the current market price. Silver cost climbs and drops like an amusement-park roller coaster. Another point regarding silver price is worth mention: Many suppliers will discount (however little) for bulk orders or quantities over a certain weight. So a price may be set for silver in weights up to 3 or 4 or 5 ounces, and less for weights between 5 and 10 ounces, and so forth.

The beginning jeweler should not be turned off by the cost of the basic working material. As expensive as silver may appear to be, it is still far below the value of a finished piece. Few other crafts cost as little in terms of equipment, tools, and space, yet return as much in satisfaction, alike to maker or wearer or viewer.

For example, the pendant shown on pages 82–91 to illustrate construction required approximately 16 inches of 12-gauge square wire, about 8 inches of 14-gauge square wire, perhaps an inch of 14-gauge round wire, and negligible amounts of solder, flux, and fuel. The cost of the wire, employing the silver-cost information, is calculated as follows: A 12-gauge square wire weighs .081 ounces per inch. This weight times the 16 inches used weighs 1.296 ounces. Multiply the 1.296 times the current cost of silver per ounce—at this writing, it is $6.66—and the cost comes to $8.63. In much the same way the cost for the 14 gauge can be figured. This wire weighs .064 ounces per inch, which times 8 inches comes to .512 ounces. Multiply the .512 times the current cost of silver ($6.66) and the result is $3.41. If you add the cost for the 12 gauge ($8.63) and the cost for the 14 gauge ($3.41), the total is $12.04. To this add a dollar or two for fuel, solder, flux, and at $13 or $14 of material, this is a good value! The other equation is time spent on making the pendant. As memory serves, this was about three hours—but this can hardly be counted as a cost, for it was pleasurable.

It should be kept in mind that silver, unlike many other craft materials (leather, rattan, fabric, or wood), cannot be destroyed so as to make it unusable. Silver can be melted, flattened, and reworked, or, indeed, sold as scrap for refining. At the very least, the craftsman can use bits and pieces and failures for casting.

Other materials are, of course, used by the jewelry craftsman. These include some which are common and inexpensive; and some rare and very expensive;

STERLING SILVER

Prices are based upon weight. When ordering sheet, the following weight approximations may be used to determine the quantity price bracket. *Note:* The figures below are the *weight* per piece in troy ounces.

Size	10 ga.	12 ga.	14 ga.	16 ga.	18 ga.
6 x 6 in.	20.10 oz.	15.95 oz.	12.60 oz.	10.05 oz.	7.95 oz.
6 x 5 in.	16.75 oz.	13.30 oz.	10.55 oz.	8.30 oz.	6.65 oz.
6 x 4 in.	13.40 oz.	10.65 oz.	8.45 oz.	6.70 oz.	5.30 oz.
6 x 3 in.	10.05 oz.	8.00 oz.	6.30 oz.	5.00 oz.	4.00 oz.
6 x 2 in.	6.70 oz.	5.35 oz.	4.20 oz.	3.35 oz.	2.65 oz.
6 x 1 in.	3.35 oz.	2.70 oz.	2.10 oz.	1.70 oz.	1.35 oz.
3 x 3 in.	5.02 oz.	3.98 oz.	3.15 oz.	2.51 oz.	1.98 oz.

Size	20 ga.	22 ga.	24 ga.	26 ga.	28 ga.
6 x 6 in.	6.30 oz.	5.05 oz.	4.00 oz.	3.15 oz.	2.55 oz.
6 x 5 in.	5.25 oz.	4.20 oz.	3.30 oz.	2.65 oz.	2.10 oz.
6 x 4 in.	4.20 oz.	3.35 oz.	2.65 oz.	2.10 oz.	1.70 oz.
6 x 3 in.	3.15 oz.	2.50 oz.	2.00 oz.	1.60 oz.	1.25 oz.
6 x 2 in.	2.10 oz.	1.70 oz.	1.35 oz.	1.05 oz.	.85 oz.
6 x 1 in.	1.05 oz.	.85 oz.	.65 oz.	.55 oz.	.45 oz.
3 x 3 in.	1.57 oz.	1.26 oz.	1.00 oz.	.78 oz.	.63 oz.

Note: The above figures are weights, not prices. To obtain the price, multiply the weight by the current price per ounce.

Use the charts below for checking weights of irregular sizes of sheet or wire:

ROUND WIRE

B&S gauge	Approx. weight per ft.
¼ in.	3.23 oz.
4 in.	2.15 oz.
6 in.	1.36 oz.
8 in.	.852 oz.
9 in.	.676 oz.
10 in.	.536 oz.
12 in.	.337 oz.
14 in.	.212 oz.
16 in.	.133 oz.
18 in.	.084 oz.
20 in.	.052 oz.
22 in.	.033 oz.
24 in.	.021 oz.

SQUARE WIRE

B&S gauge	Approx. weight per ft.
¼ in.	4.00 oz.
4 in.	2.74 oz.
6 in.	1.73 oz.
8 in.	1.085 oz.
9 in.	.861 oz.
10 in.	.682 oz.
12 in.	.429 oz.
14 in.	.269 oz.
16 in.	.169 oz.
18 in.	.107 oz.

SHEET

B&S gauge	Approx. weight per sq. in.
8 in.	.701 oz.
10 in.	.558 oz.
12 in.	.443 oz.
14 in.	.351 oz.
16 in.	.278 oz.
18 in.	.221 oz.
20 in.	.175 oz.
22 in.	.139 oz.
24 in.	.110 oz.
26 in.	.087 oz.
28 in.	.070 oz.

RECTANGULAR WIRE

B&S gauge	Approx. weight per ft.
4 x 16 in.	.684 oz.
6 x 18 in.	.426 oz.
6 x 22 in.	.266 oz.
8 x 22 in.	.210 oz.
8 x 18 in.	.300 oz.
8 x 16 in.	.450 oz.
8 x 14 in.	.535 oz.
⅛ x 20 in.	.263 oz.
11 x 20 in.	.191 oz.
14 x 18 in.	.168 oz.
⅜ x 12 in.	1.95 oz.
⅜ x 14 in.	1.60 oz.
¼ x 12 in.	1.30 oz.
¼ x 14 in.	1.05 oz.

and, as is the case with some materials (notably ivory now), some almost impossible to get in any quantity. Certain materials used may be easy to work with, such as hard woods and ivory, or some may be difficult to work with in conjunction with jewelry. This latter group would include feathers, ceramics, and leather. These require special treatment and care when used with silver, and are probably best left to the experienced craftsman.

Particularly attractive in relation to silver are ebony and ivory. A few other hard woods are also used (coco-bolo, lignum vitae, and rosewood) but they are not as easy to work, nor are they as complementary to silver. Ivory and ebony because of their solid neutral color—the stark white of ivory and the intense black of ebony—stand in attractive contrast to silver. In addition to the color factor, each "works" very much like silver. Each can be sawed, filed, sanded, and polished. Each is a valuable part of the craftsman's store pile of basic working materials. This is not to say, however, that each does not have some design and structure restrictions on its use in jewelry. Although they are dense materials, and reasonably tight-grained, that grain must be considered to avoid chipping and splitting. With ebony, because it is a wood, the grain runs in a single direction and this is best employed with a length-to-grain design: Very simply, use the grain along the length of a design. Ivory can split in a number of different ways, and, with elephant-tusk ivory, even in concentric circles. But if ivory and ebony are used as though they are soft gemstones—that is, set and supported with a reasonable degree of protection from blows—they will last as long as the silver. Ebony can benefit from an occasional oiling, done by wiping on forehead or nose!

The most widely used other materials of the jewelry craftsman are gems and decorative stones and shells. And these are very much in the province of the beginner. The classification of stones into categories labeled "precious" and "semiprecious" has been pretty much discarded. This doesn't make diamonds, rubies, emeralds, sapphires, opals, and pearls any less precious; the problem with this classification is the assumption that "precious" means of great value or expense. This is not necessarily true. A very-good-quality semiprecious stone may be much more valuable than a second-grade precious stone. The term "gemstones" covers this broad categorization more easily. In general, this includes stones that are rare, hard, usually transparent (obviously excepting pearl and opal), and which may be cut and polished. Stones that are not transparent, and which will not "hold" a faceted shape, are called "ornamental stones," although this too is subject to exceptions.

Good stones are widely accessible and surprisingly inexpensive. The jeweler/craftsman wants a stone that is of the appropriate size, shape, color, and hardness (but not brittle). The hardness of a stone is indicated by its number on a relative scale called the Mohs scale. This ranges from 1 through 10, with diamond the hardest. The minerals comprising the scale are: (1) talc, (2) gypsum, (3) calcite, (4) fluorspar, (5) apatite, (6) orthoclase, (7) quartz, (8) topaz, (9) corundum, and (10) diamond.

Relative hardness on the scale is a bit misleading, for a diamond is, in fact, three or four times harder than the next hardest mineral on the scale. The craftsman's concern is that a stone be hard enough for use—and this means in most instances about a 6 in hardness. Hardnesses less than this (or perhaps less than 5) should be avoided, unless special care is taken to set the stone in protected settings.

Stones come in a variety of shapes ranging from the convoluted forms of tumbled stones to the intricately formal hard gems to the simple oval of the cabochon cut. For the beginner simple, fairly low-crowned, easy-ovaled cabochons are probably the easiest to work with. More on this will appear in the section on setting stones, pages 58–63.

basic tools and work areas

The basic tools used in making jewelry are relatively small and comparatively inexpensive. Few cost more than a common carpenter's hammer or saw, and most cost considerably less. They tend, of course, to be compact, portable, and in almost every instance can be hand-held. A complete workshop with all the tools needed to construct a piece of jewelry can be contained in a tool kit, or an old artist's paint box, or even an attaché case.

As the beginning jeweler gains experience and skill, the amount and complexity of his equipment is likely to increase also. The same tools can be used for a variety of purposes, but with experience specific tools tend to be chosen and used for quite specific intentions. For example, a single forging hammer of 10 to 14 ounces, with a combination of faces (hitting surfaces), one face slightly domed and the other face very domed, can be employed for most of the beating a beginner will undertake. Later the craftsman will develop a feel for weight and face shape and want a more specialized hammer for particular forging results.

Although a single tool can be used for different jewelry purposes, it is possible to misuse that tool if the purposes to which it is put are radically different —or if it is used for the wrong purpose. If you are not certain, check before using the tool. Learn the names and functions of the more common tools used in the jewelry craft. Shown on page 18 are the most widely used and significant basic tools in jewelry making. They are shown in functional groupings and in a few instances with some overlap of their use. They will be discussed in detail under "Basic Techniques."

Beginning at the bottom left is the basic material: silver, in both sheet and wire form. Immediately above is a gauge measure and above that a jeweler's vise and a ring clamp. To the right of the clamp and the vise are three small jeweler's pliers, a jeweler's saw frame, and a tin snip. In the middle of the photo are a hand drill, a set of drill bits, and a punch. In the top right-hand corner resting on an asbestos slate are all the basic materials for soldering and annealing. At the very top are two glass containers, one for Sparex and one for water, with a copper tong resting on the edge of the glasses. Just below is a small hand-held butane torch. Below the torch are four small containers, one for flux and three for the principal grades of solder: hard, medium, and easy. Below these and on the bottom edge of the asbestos plate are a borax slate and a charcoal block, and on the right edge of the plate a "scratcher" for lighting the torch. On the bottom right are two small forming stakes and below these a 4 by 4 steel beating block. To the left of the block are a ring measure and a ring mandrel. Resting on the mandrel are two forming hammers. Above the two steel hammers is a fiber mallet and to the left of the mallet, in the center of the photograph, are four small needle files. To the left of the small files are three large hand-held files with a slip-on handle.

Of the tools shown, the approximate cost as of this writing (mid-1978) comes to a round figure of approximately $100 to $150. On page 19 are some breakdowns of individual items, with costs rounded off to the nearest half-dollar. *Note:* Items not absolutely necessary are shown with an asterisk. All in all, this is not an unreasonable figure with which to begin an exciting new craft. It costs much less than a set of golf clubs, ski equipment, or a new sailboat.

Working arrangements or setups for jewelry may range from a tabletop in the corner of the room to a complete craft studio. Whatever the arrangements, they evolve from the needs of the individual jeweler. It is unlikely that the working area and tool setup designed (or worked out by habit and practice) or suitable for one craftsman could satisfy another. Some craftsmen need their tools close at hand, and in precise order, with clear work space and everything contained. Others appear oblivious to apparent

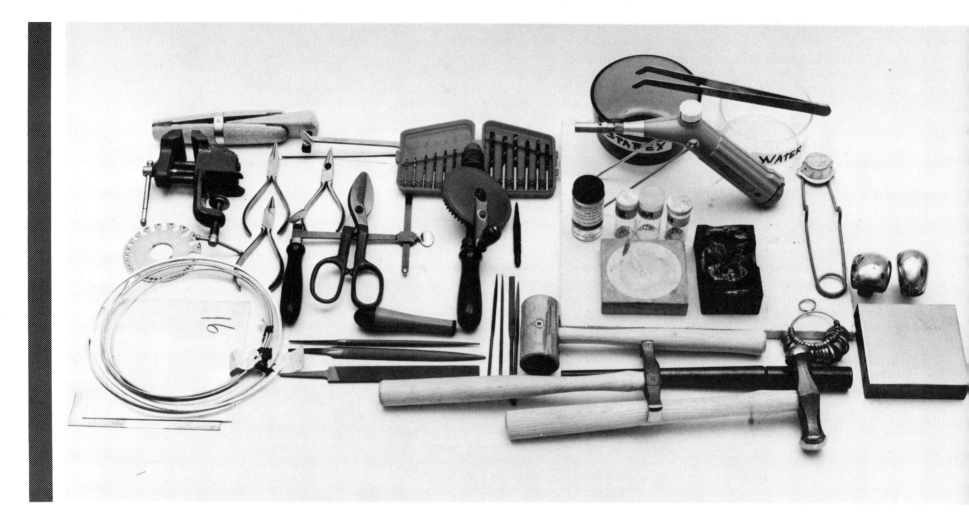

Here are all of the basic tools and, indeed, a few not absolutely essential.

APPROXIMATE COST OF TOOLS

Silver gauge	$ 8.00*	
Jeweler's vise	9.00	
Clamp	4.00	
3 pliers	18.00	(Approx. $6.00 each)
Saw frame	6.00	(Plus $3.00 for blades)
Tin snips	5.00	
Tongs	2.50	
Drill bit set	6.00*	(Buy as needed.)
Hand drill	6.00	
Punch	. . . .	(Use a nail.)
Glass containers	1.00	
Torch unit (complete)	15.00	
Scratcher	1.00	(Use matches, of course.)
Flux and solder	.50	(Price is for silver solder flux.)
Borax slate	4.50*	
Charcoal block	1.50	
2 stakes	17.00*	
Steel block	4.00	
Ring gauge	6.00*	
Mandrel	10.00	
Hammer (shallow dome)	6.50	
Hammer (deep dome)	6.50	
Fiber mallet (rawhide)	5.00	
Set of 4 files	5.00	
3 large hand files	10.00	
Handle	.50	

$153.00   And then subtracting some
—41.00   for extra (asterisked) items.
─────────
$112.00

chaos, with their tools in disarray and work surfaces cluttered with odds and ends. Yet flowing beauty can stem from the rigid working environment of one, and flawless order and jewelry perfection from the barnyard shambles of another.

Many craftsmen position their tools, for convenience, into functional groupings. Most of these groupings are obvious technique families—pliers together, hammers together, and so on. However, many groupings are not really planned as much as they reflect patterns grown out of a habit which in fact may not be very functional. Obviously, having to turn to reach a hammer, and then turn again to locate the beating base or stake, and then perhaps another turn later for annealing can be enormously time-wasting. The wise craftsman will take some time to analyze his working arrangements, assessing their functioning, positioning, and, therefore, convenience.

But as helpful as a good working arrangement can be, it is not, frankly, imperative to the production of attractive jewelry. It is important—very important—that tools be kept in good shape. This is perhaps the one thread that ties jewelry craftsmen: their respect for the tools of their trade. And with this goes their strong concern for the continued good condition of those instruments they use for their creative expression. Good tools, kept in good shape, do not guarantee quality work. But shoddy tools make shoddy work a virtual certainty.

A number of basics are meaningful for the tools used in jewelry. First, whatever the item, it must be "clean" and allowed to do the job for which it was intended. Surfaces which strike or hit metal directly and smoothly must be free of scratches, marks, indentations, and dirt. Soldering blocks should be free of bits and pieces of scrap silver and solder. Soldering brushes should be free of encrusted flux and bits of solder, as well as dirt. Indeed, some of these tools —for example, forging hammers and base plates and stakes—would benefit from being polished. Second, cutting tools should be able to cut as intended. Ridges and teeth in files and saw blades must be free of waste metal. A medium-cut file that is clogged with metal fragments is no longer a medium cut—but soon becomes a rough file.

BASIC TECHNIQUES

holding

Because the sheet silver and wire used by the jewelry craftsman is comparatively small, often thin, short, or narrow—and can be maddeningly slippery and difficult to hold by hand—a number of "holding tools" are used to assist in gripping the work. These may operate by screw, spring, leverage, or the human hand for action, but all must have a smooth face, and all must hold as firmly as the operator needs. This usually means keeping bulky fingers out of the way and allowing room for other tools. Most holding tools do their job best when the item being worked on is secured as close as possible to the gripping surface or jaws.

There are four general kinds of holding tools. A few others may be used from time to time, but the following are the most significant:

TWEEZERS AND TONGS. These may be short, long, thin, wide, thick, of wire or sheet metal, and made from copper, iron, steel, or wood. Most function simply by squeezing and thereby closing the end. A few operate by spring action and must be squeezed to open (and release). The majority are designed to pick, grip, and hold tiny fragments of virtually anything. A few are intended to hold pieces of work in position for soldering. These hold by spring action and obviously are unaffected by heat. Some others, like copper and wood, are used to retrieve silver from

Sparex because they do not react against the silver. And they are themselves not affected by the acid.

PLIERS. Jewelry pliers are intended both to hold and to provide a surface for bending reasonably narrow-gauge wire and sheet metal. Pliers are indispensable for working on tiny pieces of sheet or short lengths of wire. The gripping ends (the "nose") of pliers may vary in shape on one or both faces. That shape provides their identification. Round nose, flat nose, flat to round nose, and needle nose (sometimes called "chain nose") are the most common. The same size, and very often packaged with pliers, is a plierlike tool which in fact is a small snip for fine-wire cutting.

RING CLAMP. This tool is, uniquely, exclusive to the jewelry craftsman. A simple, traditional tool of common materials, it is doubtful its design can be matched or improved. It is made of two pieces of wood with a metal band circling the middle. This metal band keeps the two pieces together and serves as a fulcrum. A third piece of wood, wedge-shaped, by spreading one end closes the other and creates a grip. One end of the ring clamp is square-edged, the other is rounded, and the inside faces on both ends are covered with leather. From time to time these leather faces may need slight roughening with a file;

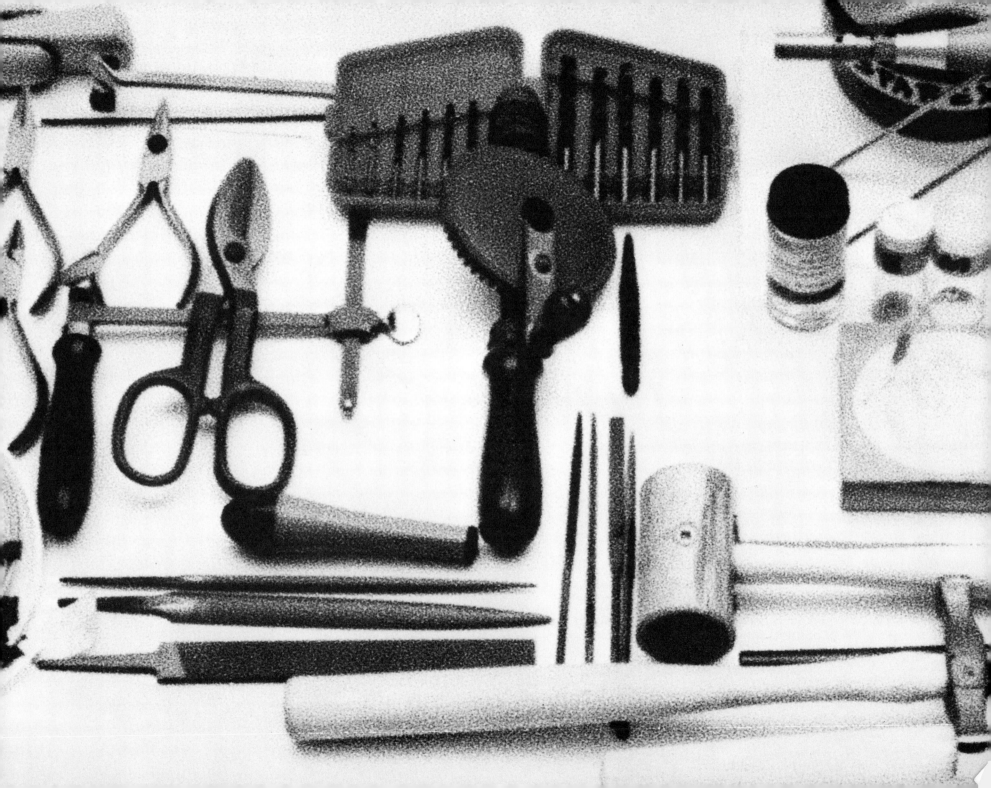

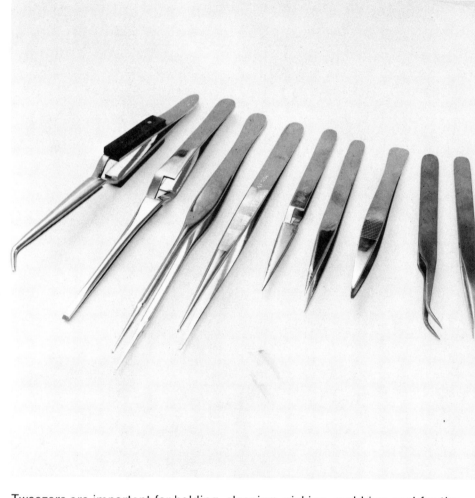

Tweezers are important for holding, clasping, picking, grabbing, and for the hundred and one things one does with silver and other small pieces in jewelry.

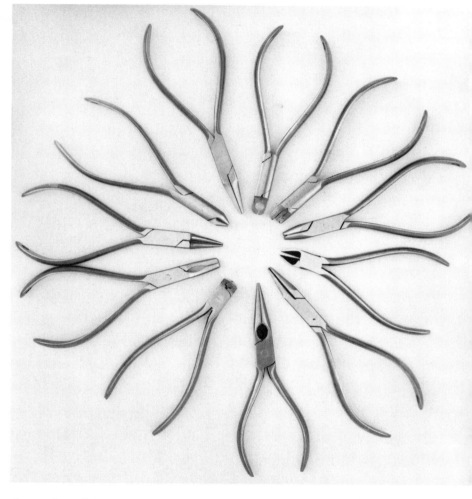

Just a few of the enormous array of different kinds of pliers available to the jewelry craftsman.

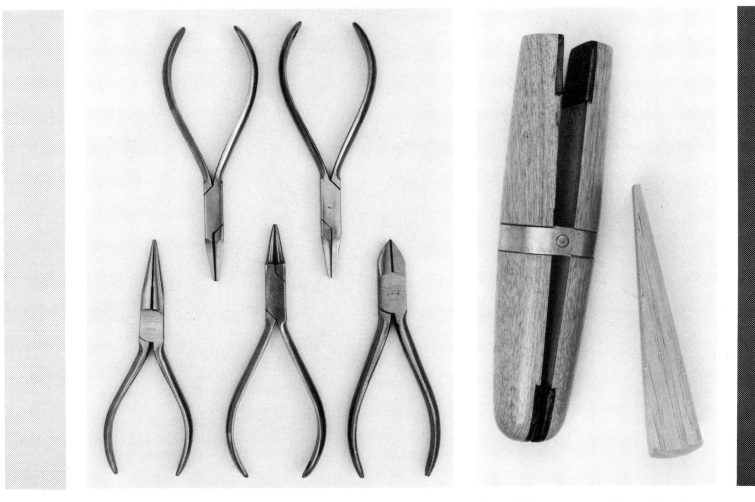

The most widely used pliers (and indeed, even including a small snip): these are the round nose, needle nose, square, and half round to square.

One of the most versatile tools in the craftsman's work chest is the ring clamp.

the leather faces can get glossy from use and lose some of their holding power. The wedge should not be jammed into place by banging on a tabletop. A much firmer grip is made by sliding it from the side —and this also saves the tool from damage.

JEWELER'S VISE. The jeweler's vise is a comparatively small unit ranging from 2 by 4 inches to 3 by 5 inches, with parallel jaws which work on a screw principle for tightening. The jaws when tightened provide a very strong grip. The most popular and common model may be clamped and tightened onto the edge of a table. Although most units come with screw holes provided in the base, few craftsmen secure them permanently. More elaborate units have swivel bases that permit the vise to be turned in a circle. And very elaborate units may have a ball-and-socket base, which permits complete freedom of movement. These units are very free in movement but tend not to be as secure as the others. Most work done with the vise doesn't justify the extra expense.

The vise operates very simply by tightening the front jaw with a screw handle to close on the back jaw. The jaws are aligned and slide along two smooth bolts which fit within the rear sleeve part. Many have an added little feature, which in all candor is not particularly helpful, and that is a small anvil on the rear part. The value of the vise lies in its tremendous grip and firm, straight metal edges. It is probably the best way to hold metal for quick filing, and straight-edged cutting with the jeweler's saw.

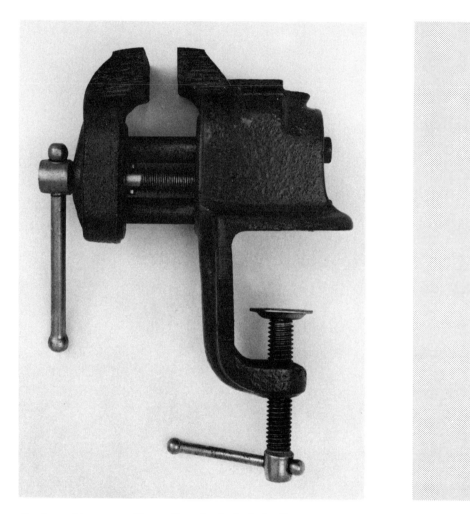

Preferred by many (the author included) for its superior holding power is the jeweler's vise.

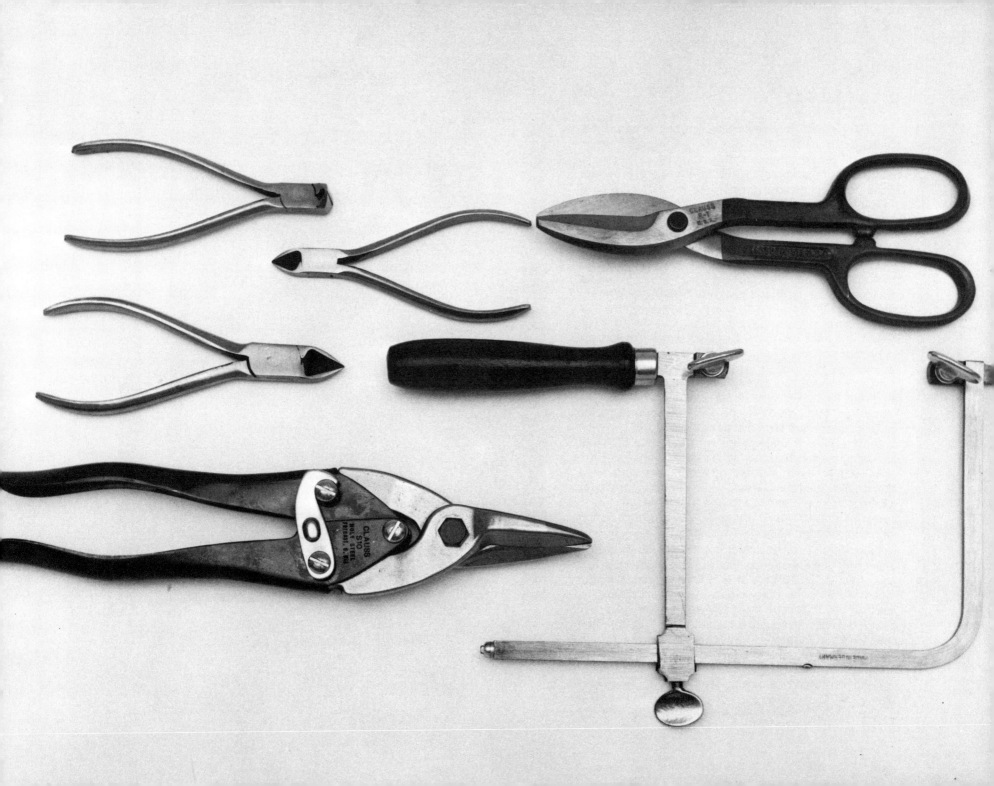

cutting

Cutting metal is a basic and frequently employed technique in jewelry. It is essential in the creation of almost all jewelry, from cutting complex patterns in flat sheets to snipping wire. In the very broadest terms, cutting generally refers to sheet silver, and snipping to wire. But were it that simple then all tools would be logically labeled "cutting" cutters and wire snips. As it is, tin snips (really cutters, although originally used for tin) are now employed to cut, not snip, sheet silver. To confuse the issue just a bit more, they may be used also for snipping wire. To add to this comedy of terminology, wire cutters, of course, are more properly labeled "snips." There are an array of available cutters (called snips, but for cutting sheets and more usually wire) and snips (called tin snips, but not really for tin, and in fact as a rule used for cutting).

At the risk of thoroughly confusing the issue, the tin snips fall into two broad categories of shape: round and straight. Yes, and generally round is for cutting round, and straight for cutting straight.

Cutting can be undertaken with a variety of tools: tin snips, wire cutters, small jeweler's snips, and the most widely used cutting tool—the jeweler's saw frame and blade(s). Most beginners use snips or cutters too small for the job at hand. If in doubt, it is better to employ snips and cutters which may be too large, for though they may be unwieldy, they will do the job. Tools that are too small will not do the work. Snips and cutters operate like scissors (on a leverage and sheer principle), so it is important to place the metal to be cut as deep within the cutter opening as possible. Also accept the fact that neither snip nor cutter is really designed to make a fine or finished cut. Most often cutters are used to merely rough-shape a piece of metal and are used only for the first, fast cut. For many jewelry craftsmen the use of snips is confined to merely cutting (snipping) solder to bit sizes.

The jeweler's saw frame with blades is clearly the

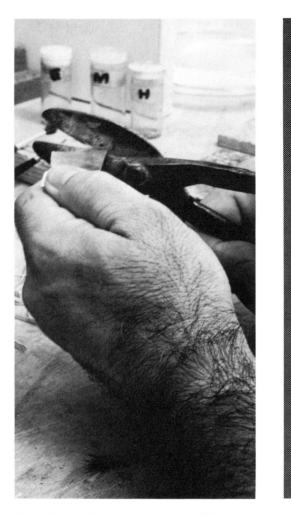

Tin snips cutting. A very powerful scissorslike tool for cutting sheet and wire.

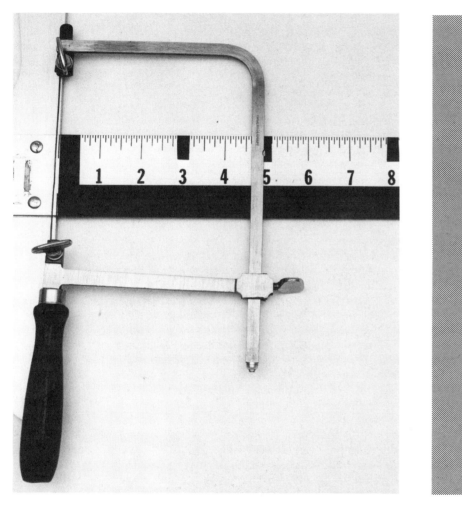

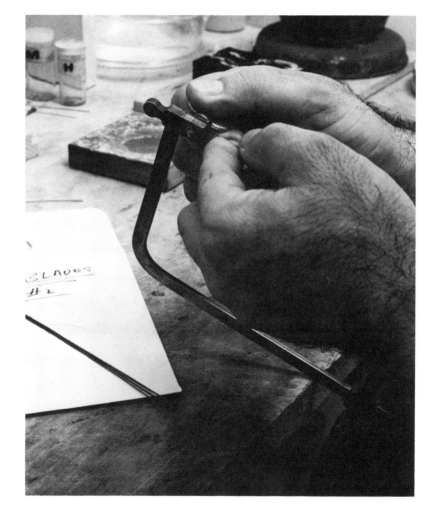

The jeweler's saw frame. Shown is the 5-inch depth. The frame can be gotten with both 3-inch openings or as deep as 8-inch. But 5 inches seems to be the most convenient for the beginner.

Setting the blade in the frame begins with the blade teeth held facing down to the handle and out of the opening: DOWN AND OUT. The top set screw is then tightened.

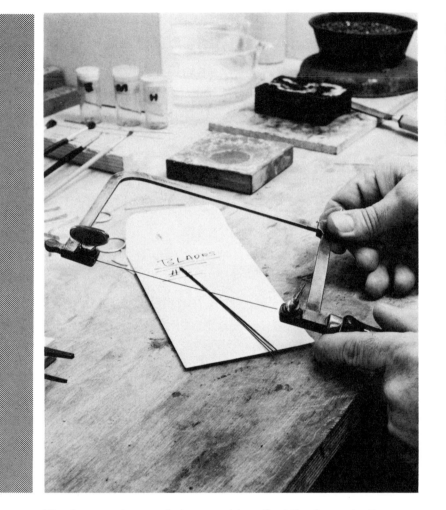

The frame set screw is loosened to adjust the frame to the blade length, then tightened.

most versatile and widely used metal-cutting tool. The saw frame itself is available in a number of sizes (or really depths of cut) and in grades of quality. Quality of frame is not, frankly, a very important consideration; depth of cut is. Imagine the letter C (reversed, and more of this in a moment) with a handle at the bottom. Then imagine that this form can be made taller or shorter; that's the adjustable part of the frame, and it is moved to accommodate the saw blade. The depth of the frame is the measure from the end, or opening, of the C to the back side. That is not adjustable, and unless you know that you are liable to have reason to cut long, long pieces, then get and use a short frame. The sizes range from 3 inches to 8 inches and the middle size of about 5 inches is the most convenient.

The frame has three set screws. One is at the top, another is opposite at the bottom and near the handle, and the third is at the bottom back side of the frame. The bottom back set screw is used to set the opening for the saw blade, and the remaining two are to secure the blade (one of these, usually the bottom, after the blade has been positioned in place, puts the frame and the secured blade under tension). The blade is set with the teeth facing down to the handle and out of the opening. The phrase is: DOWN AND OUT. In the sequence shown, the blade is positioned into the jaws at the top of the saw frame, and the teeth are facing down and out. The screw is then tightened. The next set screw—the one at the bottom rear—is then loosened to adjust the size of the opening (and, of course, for the length of the blade —and the blade should not *quite* fit). This set screw is then tightened. Now, before the blade can be fitted within the jaws at the last and bottom front set of jaws, the frame must be sprung to allow the blade to sit. This last set screw is then tightened. The frame

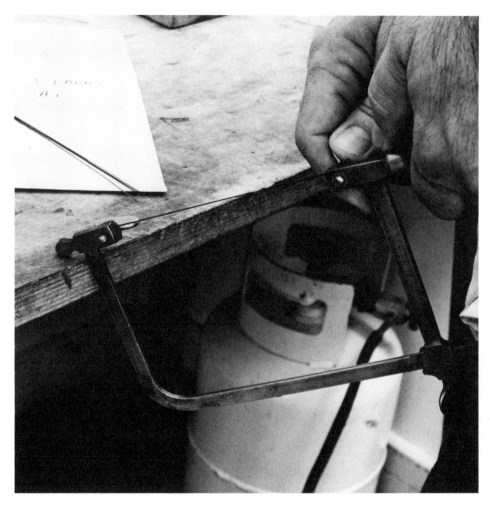

The bottom set screw is then tightened.

To saw, the metal is held firmly and the frame lightly. The metal should be cut on a pull stroke. Here it is shown on a bench pin.

is ready to use. A way to test the blade—for it must be under tension—is to "pluck" it with the fingers. The resulting sound should be a high "ping." A "thunking" sound means a loose blade, and means a broken blade will shortly follow. Remember, it is almost impossible to set the blade in too tight or with too much tension.

Blade sizes for the jeweler's saw frame range in thickness (cut) from quite large and rough for wood and very heavy metal sawing, to very fine for cutting bezels and fine wire. These sizes are of course relative. The heaviest blade is still finer than coarse thread. The finest blade is so fine that the teeth are hard to see. Blades are sized by number from number 6, the roughest cut, through 5, 4, 3, 2, and 1 to 1/0, 2/0, 3/0, 4/0, 5/0, 6/0, and 7/0 (the finest). The medium range is the most widely used: numbers 2, 1, 1/0, 2/0, and 3/0.

The size of a blade and the cut it takes reflect in turn the number of teeth per inch. The greater the number per inch of blade, the smaller they have to be, with the result that the blade is both thinner and, with more teeth, finer. To the untrained eye, these differences are small indeed. Develop the habit of keeping blades separated and identified by number or cutting action—very rough, rough, medium, fine, very fine, and so on.

The size of the blade to use for cutting depends on more than one factor; the thickness of the metal is the most important. Many schemes have been devised for determining the appropriate size of blade (two teeth per thickness, for example). But all of these are difficult calculations to make with blades closely resembling human hair. Until some feel for blade cut is established, it is much easier to simply use a smaller blade. Working with a smaller blade means only that the cutting takes longer. If the saw frame and blade "chatter" or snag on the metal, then the blade is too large. On the other hand, if the cutting seems to be going all right but taking a long time, then use a larger blade. Whatever the thickness of the metal, if it requires fine, detailed cutting, then a smaller blade must be used.

The cutting process itself is very simple, provided the beginner holds to a few simple maxims. The

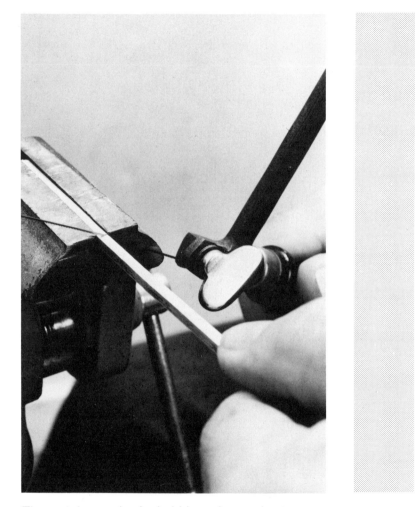

The metal may also be held in a vise, and cut on an angle, or even sideways. This photo shows well how relatively small the blade is in relation to the metal being cut.

single most important of these is to hold the metal firmly. This means in most instances that the metal must be cut as close as possible to the supporting tool. Most cutting actions require the saw frame and blade to be at right angles to the metal. Later, with more skill, there will be times when the jeweler deliberately cuts at an angle. Holding the frame lightly, keep in mind that the *teeth are down and out* of the frame. Cutting takes place only on the pull stroke. The saw frame and the action should feel as though the frame and blade are sliding up the metal and being pulled, and cutting on the down stroke. Vigorous cutting simply wastes half the motion.

The beginner should consider broken blades as part of the learning experience—up to a point. If more than a dozen blades have been broken in the first few hours of cutting (and learning), then something is drastically wrong. Check for the following: (1) Technique—is the saw frame held properly, and is the frame being held loosely? (2) Is the proper blade size being used (too large, it will snag; too small, it may twist and break)? And (3) is the metal to be cut being held firmly?

Some hints: Don't bother waxing blades. This widely recommended practice takes more time than it is worth, and can, in fact, clog the teeth of small blades. On the other hand, do take the time to cut and paste a paper form on the silver as a guide for cutting. The reason for the paper form is simply that it stays secure, and is easier to see for cutting. With pencil or pen marks these can smudge. And also the paper form gives a better picture of the piece being cut, and can be left for some time on the piece as a protective covering, and as a guide for filing. The paper form is simply glued on the back side and adhered to the silver.

With use, blades will not break—but they do get dull. When this happens, simply throw them away. If the cutting action seems to be taking an unusually long time, then use a larger blade—or change blades. When cutting a straight line, use as large a blade as possible, for its thickness tends to serve as its own guide. And finally, do not cut when you can file, and most assuredly do not file when you can, and should, cut.

drilling

Drilling through metal is an important technique in jewelry making because this basic skill has so many reasons for being done. A hole may be drilled to hold a rivet for a catch, to make a slide opening, to set various materials (ivory, wood, etc.), to hold design pegs, and in order to make a hole to pass a saw blade through for inside cutting. The drilling technique may also be employed to drill partway through a piece of silver—making an "almost" hole for design purposes. And last, a hole may be drilled to correct a mistake. For example, if a hole has been drilled too large or in the wrong location, it may be drilled again, to be larger, then filled with the appropriate size wire, soldered, and redrilled. And too, a hole may be necessary to push out a stone from a "bezel setting" (drilling from the backside). The stone is pushed out, the hole is filled with wire and resoldered, and of course the stone reset.

The tools involved in drilling include a hand (or powered) drill, drill bits, a punch of some kind (this could be a nail), and an old hammer for the punch. There are two reasons for the punch: It serves to mark the precise spot to be drilled, and more importantly it serves to hold the drill bit in place in order to drill. Without the tiny burred edge the punch creates, the drill bit would roll or wander over the surface and not "catch" an edge. The punch should not be hit with the face of a forging hammer, for this will ruin that tool's smooth polished surface.

An inexpensive hand drill is all that is necessary. More elaborate models do not perform any better. A flexible-shaft powered drill is more convenient, but has little else to recommend it for drilling only. Drill bits range in size from tiny needlelike bits to what is, for jewelry, quite large at 1/4 inch. If holes larger than this are needed, then it is necessary first to drill a hole large enough to pass a saw blade through, then rig the saw and cut the opening.

Drill bits are typically ordered by a number size. The smaller (lower) the number, the thicker the drill bit, and of course the larger the hole made. The measuring system is very much like the system used with metal. Indeed, certain drill bits correspond in thickness to specific gauge sizes of metal (and, of course, wire). As examples: 10 gauge corresponds to bit number 37; 12 gauge to number 46; 14 gauge to number 50; 16 gauge to number 55; 18 gauge to number 58; 20 gauge to number 67; 24 gauge to number 75; and 26 gauge to number 78.

Drilling is very easy. The only problem may lie in the natural assumption that because it is so easy anyone can do it. Anyone *can* do it, provided he or she follows a few simple steps.

First, mark where the hole is to be located, and this should not be a blurred approximation with a heavy pencil.

Be sure you have the metal resting on a metal base before attempting the next step. With the silver on a base, hold a punch (an old nail or a good sharp-pointed punch or ice pick) on the precise spot marked. Tap the punch smartly with a small carpenter's hammer, not a forming hammer. This will create a slight indentation and a burred edge to enable the drill bit to catch and not wander over the surface of the smooth metal. Before the actual drilling, transfer the piece to be drilled to a wooden support. From this comes the admonition TAP ON METAL, DRILL ON WOOD. Next, secure the bit firmly within the chuck (end) of the drill. Be sure the piece to be drilled is held in place on the scrap wood, by taping or holding to an edge. If this is not done, the piece may turn with the drill bit. Place the bit carefully on the dapped spot, and begin to turn the drill han-

The spot to be drilled is marked precisely, with a pen or pencil.

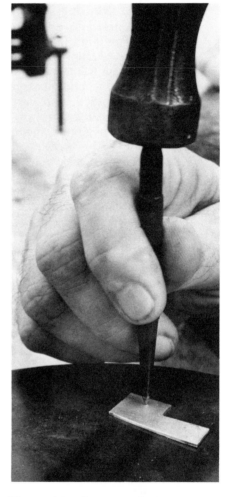

Then with a hammer, but not a forming hammer, the spot is tapped smartly to create a burred edge. This edge prevents the drill bit from "wandering."

dle *slowly*. It is not necessary to spin the drill rapidly. In fact, if turned too rapidly it may not cut but simply spin on top of the metal. Most drilling is done at right angles to the metal or wood, but it can be done at other angles. And too, most drilling is through a piece, but there may be times when it is desirable to stop before opening through.

The final step in drilling is to file and finish the burr edge, particularly on the back side of the hole.

If the hole being drilled is for a rivet, then it becomes important to clamp the pieces being drilled until all holes have been drilled—or provide for temporary holding wires or rivets. The reason, of course, is to prevent the pieces from shifting position and misaligning the holes already drilled. In making rivet holes be sure to check drill-bit size and rivet size. The rivet should fit snugly and not have excessive play. A craft trick in this regard is to drill the hole to size, then with a very, very large drill bit provide a countersink. This is a cone-shaped opening at each end. Then when the rivet is tapped in place, it spreads to fill this opening. This creates a wedge-like form locking both ends in securely. One final hint: If in doubt as to size, make it smaller and then ream it open with a round needle file. A hole too large is a nuisance to make smaller (filling in, soldering, filing flush, and then redrilling).

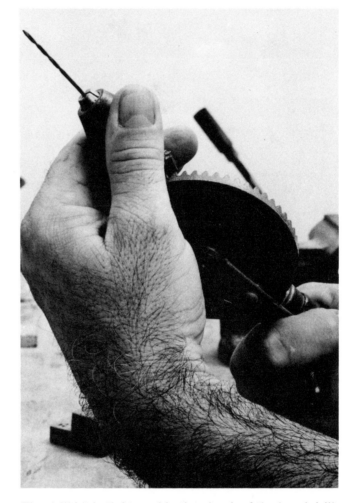

The drill bit is tightened in the chuck of the hand drill.

The drill bit is placed on the punched mark and the handle of the drill is turned slowly.

filing

Filing is employed to smooth rough edges which may result from drilling, cutting, or hammering. Files are also used to "true" straight edges, shape irregular curves, and remove slight amounts of unwanted metal—amounts so small that cutting is not justified. In practice, files are also used to shape two pieces or edges in preparation for soldering. Note that the file is rarely used across the face of a sheet of silver, because it would groove the sheet.

Filing is probably the easiest basic process to learn. Rarely is a piece filed too much—more often it is filed too hard, but not properly. Files are designed to scratch metal, and good technique simply creates successively smaller and finer cross-scratches. Basically, one goes from a large, rough-cut file to a small, fine file. One should think in terms of stages. Skipping an intermediate stage tends to show up in the finished piece when, after polishing, scratches can be seen.

Files vary in three distinct ways: size, shape, and "cut."

SIZE. Sizes of files range from 8 to 9 inches plus handle to slightly over 3 inches overall. The file may have its abrasive (cutting) surface along its length, or the cut may be on just one side or edge, or end. In general, file size is referred to as "large hand" (8 inches plus handle), or simply "needle" (which is small—3 to 6½ inches overall without handle); also included in this classification are a number of similarly small needle files referred to as (1) jeweler's,

Files come in a great variety of sizes, shapes, and "cuts."

Here are only a dozen and a half of the many kinds of riffle files (and shapes) available to the jewelry craftsman.

which are simply a smaller version of the typical needle file, and (2) Swiss, which refers to the high quality of the steel in the file. And finally there is a classification of needlelike files called "riffle." These are specially shaped files designed to reach hard-to-get-at places—insides, edges, corners, and so forth. These come, in addition to their overall shape, with cutting actions confined to edges, sides, points, or only the very ends. They are available in literally hundreds of shapes.

SHAPE. File shapes range from flat to round and virtually every shape in between. Some of the more popular shapes are: square, round, half-round, triangular, rattail, and combinations of these. Needle files also have special shapes varying from round to flat to square and a host of forms in between.

"CUT." The roughness of a file is called its "cut." This is the combination of (1) height of teeth—more importantly the number of teeth (per inch)—and, as a consequence, the (2) space between and the number of rows of teeth. For example, a rough number-0 cut (and more of this in a moment) file may have as few as 50 or so teeth per inch. A fine number-4 cut file, on the other hand, may have three times as many teeth—or 150 per inch. One other point is worth mentioning. Files may have more than one row (although never more than two). The cutting action on large files is referred to both by name and by number—although, increasingly, number alone is a more convenient reference. The "names" of cutting actions are: rough, coarse, middle, halfway, bastard, second cut, smooth, and superfine. Cuts by number, which is virtually the only way to refer to the cutting action on small files, range from number 00, very rough, to numbers 0, 1, 2, 3, 4, 5, and 6, which last is very fine in cutting action. However, in practice you will find that numbers 0, 2, and 4 are the only ones really necessary.

Metal to be filed should be held firmly in a ring clamp or vise. A handle for files (the simple slip-on kind) is a great assist and a wise safety factor; you should use one. If a file is used without a handle, be absolutely sure you keep the end out of the palm of your hand. With the use of the ring clamp, place the part to be filed as close to the edge of the jaws in the clamp as possible. Push the wedge in tightly (and learn to slide the wedge from the side for an even tighter grip—without weakening the middle band). Do not tap the clamp wedge—this may make the jaws tighten well, but it also guarantees a short life for the clamp. With the piece to be filed secure in the clamp, then brace the clamp on a support (or even in the wedge opening of a bench pin).

The ring clamp allows work to be moved easily, repositioned, and tightened quickly, but it does require a strong, firm hold for working. The jeweler's vise is less maneuverable (limited essentially to vertical clamping actions), but it is more secure in its grip and does provide a straight edge for filing (and cutting). For most work, many craftsmen prefer it to the ring clamp.

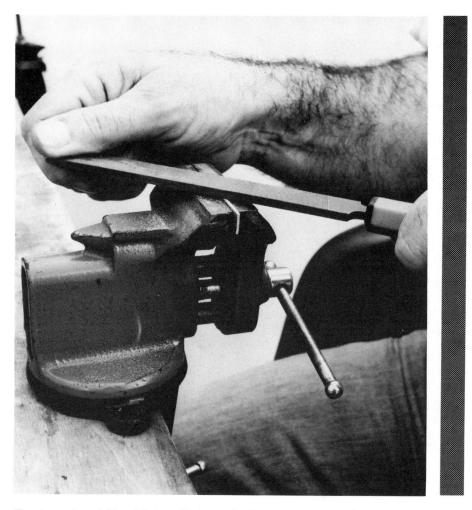

The large hand file with handle is pushed over the edge of the metal being held in a jeweler's vise.

On inside surfaces the round or half-round file is used.

And on small pieces the needle files are employed.

In general, the larger and rougher the area to be filed, the larger and rougher the file to be used. A flat file is used on outside or convex curves and, of course, on flat surfaces. A round file, along with an oval (and the round file or half-round file) is used with inside and converse curves. For tight corners, and on intricate forms, the needle files or contoured riffle files should be used. In filing, develop the habit of making smooth strokes, varying the angle and pushing the file. By all means, avoid setting up grooves in the metal. Try to cover as much metal at one time as possible—particularly when filing a straight edge. To file a straight edge it is possible to reverse the usual process by laying the file flat, and then holding the metal vertically on edge and pulling along. Be sure to change the files as needed, using progressively finer files, and do not use too rough a file to start with. Finally, file marks should not be visible when the filing is finished—all that should be discernible is a sheen of very fine abrasive marks.

Files can be kept in working condition by lightly tapping them on edge when working—to dislodge bits of metal fragments. It is also a wise practice to clean the file with a file brush—which is simply a metal-bristled brush—before using. Another hint for working with files is to mark them in some easily identified way. If the middle-cut files—such as the number 2—are marked with a wrapping of tape, this spots them and makes it easier to see the number 0 and number 4, which are *obviously* different from each other, if not very different from the number 2. Incidentally, from time to time wipe the faces of the ring clamp with a file to roughen the leather jaws and help keep them from slipping.

For tiny spots and at hard-to-reach places the shaped riffle files are used.

bending

Bending silver, as distinct from beating (forging), is the process that changes the direction of the metal. A surprising amount of bending can be accomplished simply by pushing or pulling by hand. Heavy metal requires heavier tools and strong supports.

Most craftsmen consider the tools used in bending as "soft," because they are in contrast to the hard metal used in forging hammers and plates. The hammers used in bending include ones of fiber, leather, rubber, and to some extent wood and plastic. In addition to these tools used to hit the metal, there are some specialized tools used to help shape (and also employed in forging) the metal: mandrels, stakes, and so on. (More on these later.) Anything may be used which serves to support the metal and counter the hitting/pushing action.

Bending metal should not, in practical terms, temper it, or make it unworkably stiff. However, continued working—or hitting—will impart some stiffness, and may require annealing (explained on pages 50–51). Bending should be planned with care in order not to have to undo bends. And sharp bends are particularly hard to remove from the metal.

Wire and sheet differ in the ways they may be bent. Wire is more flexible and can undertake compound directional turns and twists. Sheet silver, however, doesn't grant this same freedom. Certain shapes once made do not then allow for forging. And, too, sheet or wire once forged may prevent bending later.

One technique that is a minor extension of bending is wire twisting. In order to do this in its simplest form, a single length of wire is looped and its ends secured in a vise. The loop end is held by a hook (a bent nail works fine) secured in the chuck of a drill. Then by pulling the wire taut and turning the handle, the wire turns, or twists, on itself. This creates a complex weave of wire—not unlike a rope. More complex twists can be achieved by using different-gauge wire, or with combinations of different-shape wires.

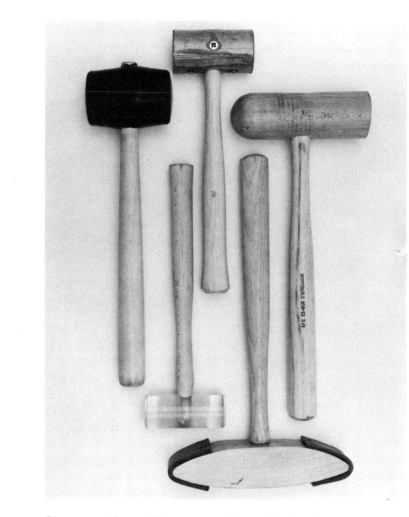

Shown are the mallets commonly used in bending.

Thinner gauges of sheet and wire can be bent, or pushed by hand.

Heavier gauges require the use of a rawhide or fiber mallet.

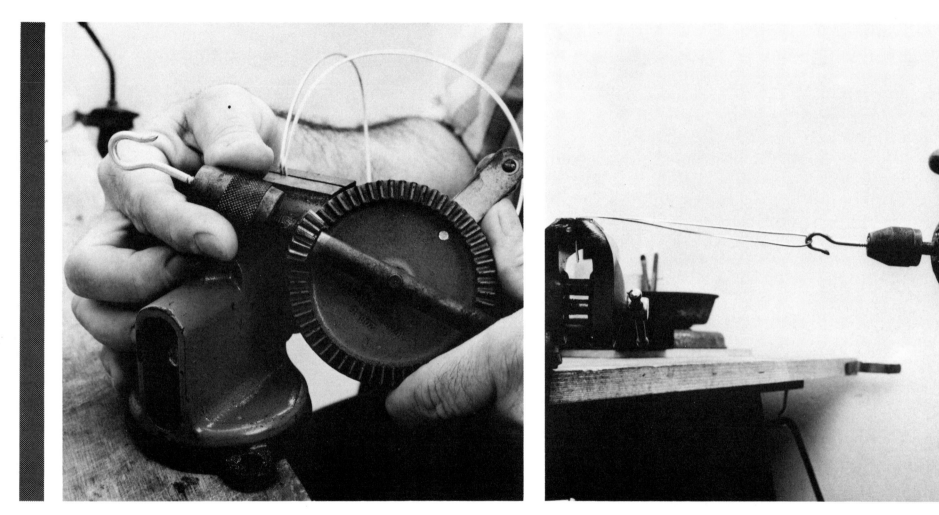

As shown on these pages, wire is held tightly in a vise with the loop end out and free.

A hook or bent nail (secured in the chuck of a hand drill) is slipped through the opening and the loop pulled tight.

As the drill handle is turned, the wire twists.

The finished, twisted wire.

beating

Beating or forming, or forging—and the words are used interchangeably—is the process by which silver's basic form is changed. The silver is hammered, or beaten, on a metal plate and is structurally altered as a consequence. The process is different from bending in that beating requires polished heavy hammers (and a metal base), usually a great number of controlled blows, and annealing (softening the metal) during the process. By beating, metal may be flattened, widened, and lengthened. In beating it is particularly important to have all working surfaces smooth. Any imperfections on a hammer face or on the surface of the base plate are transferred to the silver being worked. For this reason it is a good policy to actually polish hammers and plates from time to time.

The base on which metal may be beaten can be as simple as a polished steel block 1 inch thick by 4 by 4 inches. This base plate may be larger or smaller, and it can be found in virtually every conceivable shape or curved surface and form. Metal support bases fall into a couple of categories labeled, in general terms, either "mandrels" or "stakes." Mandrels come in three basic categories. The largest is the wrist (bracelet), then the finger, and then very small bolt-like forms from as small as one-eighth of an inch to one-half inch thick. These smaller sizes are used for wrapping wire around to make jump rings, basically, or as an aid in bending. The ring and bracelet mandrels are simply long-tapered shafts of steel designed to fashion rings and bracelets. The ring mandrels are even graduated in ring sizes.

The second major category of base for forging is the stake. Stakes are metal forms available in literally hundreds of shapes and sizes, from small teaspoon-size forms (yes, for shaping teaspoons) to rather large-winged and tapered forms as long as 3 to 4 feet in length. The shapes range from simple dome forms to convoluted scallop configurations and curved and tapered stems.

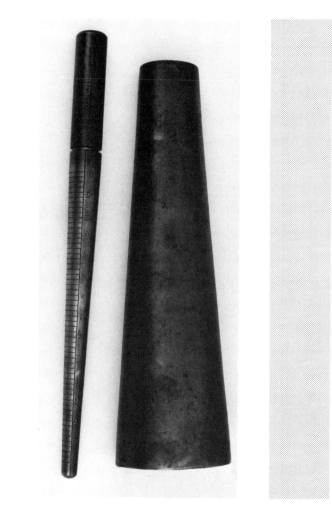

The two most common and widely used mandrels. The larger is the bracelet and the smaller is the ring mandrel.

There is no rule dictating which stake or which hammer to use for beating, aside from the admonition ROUND TO FLAT, OR FLAT TO ROUND (more about this in a following paragraph). The size of the plates and the size of the hammers will seem obvious after a bit of experience. Do not feel obliged as a beginner to use all the plates available, and certainly do not feel obligated to invest in any more than one or two base plates. A flat base plate, a ring mandrel, and perhaps a shallow-domed stake are all that is necessary to start.

The beating process, while it simply entails hammering the silver, does require some decisions—from size of hammer to the shape and configuration of both hammer and face and base plate. Also, an enormous number of craft decisions are needed: how hard to hit, in what places, and of course, for what form. A good memory jog for hammer and base plate is that easy phrase ROUND TO FLAT, OR FLAT TO ROUND. In translation: Use a round-face hammer working with a flat plate or a flat-face hammer on a round base or stake. How round or flat the face of the hammer should be depends on a number of factors. In general, the less round the face of the hammer the easier it is to control—but the slower the forging process. For the beginner, a very round face on the hammer may just work too fast for reliable control. On the other hand, too flat a face can easily create unwanted dimples or hammer ridge marks. In brief, begin with an easy-domed face and work more slowly and more carefully in the beginning.

Beating silver stiffens (tempers) it, and this obliges the craftsman to soften (anneal) the metal in order to return it to its malleable state. Failure to do this, as frequently as necessary, not only makes the metal hard to work but makes it fragile and liable to fracture. Annealing means applying heat to the stiff metal until it reaches a dull red color. The piece is then quenched in Sparex and washed in water, which both cleans and cools it, making it ready for continued working. The frequency with which the metal must be annealed is one of those abstract variables gained from experience. Very simply, the metal being worked should be annealed whenever required—and this usually means when it "feels" as if it needs

And now ROUND TO FLAT. A round hammer is used on a flat stake.

A simple method of keeping in mind an easy way to learn to "forge" is to remember to work ROUND TO FLAT, OR FLAT TO ROUND. In this photo a flat-faced hammer is used on a round stake.

Notice in this close-up shot of four faces how they range from flat face on the right through degrees to round face at the top.

it. When silver is tempered, the metal will not shape easily, it is harder to make an impression, and it feels stiff physically. If you are in doubt about the condition of the metal, then without a doubt anneal. (The process of annealing is covered in detail in the next section, and noted here because it is such an integral part of the forging process. Silver may be worked and annealed and worked and annealed continuously.) Incidentally, many craftsmen leave their work with a temper to it when they are finished in order to keep it stiff and prevent any snag from deforming the piece.

The hammers employed in beating may have an enormous range in size, weight, and type of face. Faces of hammers, or the hitting surface of the hammer, may measure from a small ½ inch to the popular sizes measuring about 1¼ inches to the large hammers of 3 to 4 inches across the hitting surface. Weights can vary from 2 to 5 ounces for what is considered a small hammer, to 8 to 10 ounces for medium-weight hammers, to 14 to 16 ounces for heavier but still medium weight, to what is considered heavy at 2 to 4 pounds. The shape of the surface will range from flat to round, and may be thin and long, or simply bulbous.

Metal-working hammers can be classified into categories of usage: forging, forming, raising, planishing, chasing, and riveting. There is, of course, some overlap in these uses, but for protracted use the hammer of the proper category makes the most sense. For example, one could(!) tap a rivet with a heavy forging hammer, but it is not easy, and there is the risk of flattening the whole piece. In general, the above categories are in the order of hammer weight. The heaviest hammers tend to be forging, the smallest used are for riveting. Forging hammers are usually large and are designed to reshape metal rapidly and dramatically. Forming hammers are for smaller work, and are probably the most widely used size for jewelry work. Raising hammers are, for the most part, the work tool of the silversmith in making compound forms which stem from the metal being stretched. The unusual shapes simply reflect this need to reach into awkward spots. Planishing hammers are simply intended to impart a faceted plane or surface to metal. Chasing hammers are used with chasing tools, which in turn hit the metal for texture and incidental shaping. Rivet hammers are, of course, the small items for setting tiny rivets, and pin backs, and stones, if used very very carefully.

The type of hammer to be used depends on the job, and often will seem almost obvious. For example, large hammers must be used to have any effect on heavy-gauge metal. Shallow-domed hammers should be used when working carefully on a controlled forging. The beginner can get by with a limited number of hammers—indeed, two should probably cover most beating intentions for the beginner. The first hammer investment for the beginner should be one with a very shallow face on one side and a very domed face on the other and which weighs about 14 to 16 ounces.

A convenient-size beating plate should be about 4 inches by 4 inches by 1 inch thick. Larger plates really are not necessary and plates any smaller are virtually useless for any serious forging. Incidentally, an old sledgehammer head or an old stove-heated flatiron (now antiques) work very well as plates.

The beginner ought to begin forging with a shallow-domed hammer. The hammer is held naturally and it should be allowed to fall naturally. It should not be "pushed" onto the metal. Where the hammer hits, the metal is forced away from that point—virtually in all directions. This increases the length of the metal, however imperceptibly, in all directions. And of course, the metal is made thinner. The beginner often overlooks these simple but obvious facts, and having hit (and moved) metal from one spot to another, then hits again in such a way that the metal is returned to the same spot. If the forging process is thought of as similar to squeezing toothpaste from a tube, it is then apparent that it must be a consistent pattern of beating or squeezing in order to force metal in a controlled direction.

The first few blows of a forging hammer on silver may surprise the beginner. Silver is easily flattened, but frustrating in the obstinacy with which it seems to want to go its own way. The metal, particularly wire, tends to turn in the same direction because the craftsman is probably hitting it, quite unconsciously, to one side only. The solution is very simple:

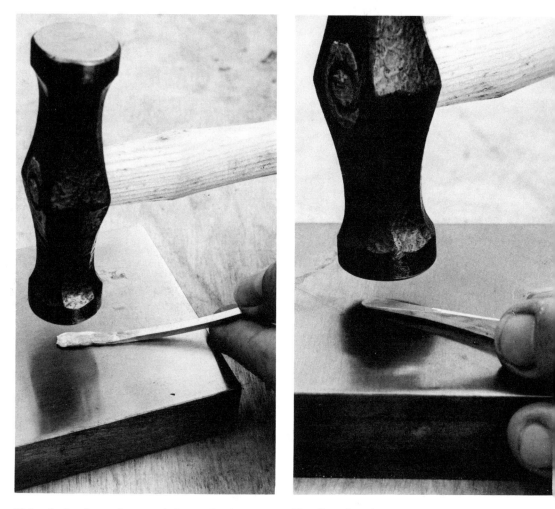

This photo shows how metal may be formed in one direction—and formed in another. Done well, the change in form should not be discernible.

The first few forming strokes will doubtless create a rough-looking surface. With experience, this is done more smoothly, and the flattening is easier.

Turn the piece over and work from the back side. And of course, the other solution is to become very conscious of the beating process and try to control the movement. Obviously, as the metal is being beaten, one side, if hit more, is spreading faster and causes the metal (with that edge now longer) to bend around —much like the outside of a curve. A good memory jog in this event is to STAY TO THE INSIDE. Simply, this means to then hit on the inside of bends.

After some practice and skill have been achieved, the beginner should attempt compound forging— and forging in combinations with bending. Compound forging, as the term is used here, means simply that the silver is beaten in such a way that it changes form radically (and yet smoothly). For example, a piece of wire would be forged going from flat in one direction or plane, to flat in an opposite (at right angles) plane. And this change in configuration would not be perceptible at any point along the entire length. Forging with bending means that the forging is done on one side of a plane, and then as the plane is changed by bending, the forging changes to continue that plane, or opposite to it.

One helpful tool used in the forging process is the dapping block, along with accompanying daps. About 4 inches square, it resembles a large dice cube. Made of steel, it has a number of large and small circular-domed depressions on each face. The daps which work with it are steel pins with ball-shape ends. These fit into the depressions, corresponding to size. A piece of silver (usually a circle, but it need not be) is placed over the appropriate depression. That is to say, the disk of metal is usually within the edge of the depression. The dap of the right size— and obviously smaller than the depression—is then held in position centered over the piece of metal. It is then rapped smartly with a hammer, *but not a forging hammer* (to use a forging hammer would guarantee its being destroyed by scarring its face). Use a regular carpenter's hammer. The piece of silver is thereby forced into the depression, or hole, and becomes cupped. Depending on how heavy the metal is, the dap may have to be hit a few times. And of course, two dapped disks can be fitted together to make a ball of silver when soldered together.

This sequence shows how the dapping block is used. First the block, and the daps with hammer. Next, a circle of metal is cut and placed within an appropriate domed depression. This is then rapped and forced into the depression. The result is a dome of metal. The ends or edge may then be filed.

annealing

Annealing is the process by which metal is returned to its malleable state after it has been worked by beating or bending. When worked, the metal becomes stiff and hard, or "tempered." Annealing is the opposite of tempering, and is absolutely necessary if the metal is to be worked upon for continuous forging. If the metal is not annealed frequently, it is not only hard to affect or change in shape, but it is very liable to crack or fracture.

Annealing requires heat—therefore a torch, and some heat-containing support. A charcoal block will work, but a pan filled with pumice or Carborundum is easier to work with and more convenient. In addition, a container of Sparex and another container of water, along with tongs of copper or wood to remove the annealed item from the Sparex bath, are needed. Strictly speaking, the Sparex quench is not necessary, but it is a traditional and convenient method to cool the work off quickly.

When it has been determined that the piece requires annealing—and this state is really more a sensed condition than any precise or exact state of the metal—then anneal. A feel for the need to anneal will come when the metal seems to be harder to shape and form. It means the metal is almost impossible to bend. If you are not certain about the temper of the metal, then by all means anneal. WHEN IN DOUBT—ANNEAL.

The piece should be placed in the annealing pan, and a torch applied. The flame should provide a wide, "bushy," and comparatively low or "soft" heat. Most craftsmen pass the torch over the whole piece, heating slowly. And most craftsmen try to anneal in an area of subdued light in order to see the color of the metal. The most reliable and easy way of gauging the condition of the metal is to observe its color as it is heated. When it turns to a dull cherry-red color, it is annealed. Be careful not to overheat the metal. After it is annealed, it is then quenched in the Sparex (most often simply by dropping it into the solution). It is retrieved with a pair of copper or wooden tongs. (The reason for using copper or wooden tongs is to prevent the copper in the metal from being drawn to the surface and discoloring it if some other metal is used to withdraw the silver.) *One other point:* If the metal is heavy or large, do not quench immediately; wait two to three seconds, for it is possible to "fracture" the silver by the sudden change of temperature. After being taken from the Sparex bath, the silver is washed in water, dried, and the work on it continues.

Because the tempering and hardening of metal can result from easy taps of the hammer, try not to hit so lightly that the metal is just being tempered and not forged. The experienced jewelry craftsman realizes that annealing is necessary, but it is also time-consuming. While he does not hesitate to anneal when he must, he also tries to avoid practices that temper more than forge.

soldering

Soldering is a process by which metal pieces are joined. For all intents and purposes, soldering fuses the piece together. If done properly, the solder joint is invisible to the naked eye. And done properly, the joint or pieces joined become as one in strength. A good solder connection is as strong as the piece as a whole.

Soldering is employed to: (1) join pieces for design purposes, (2) join pieces together as physical elements (which may or may not be a design concern), (3) secure the ends of a wire (such as for a ring or loop), (4) add a piece, and (5) affix findings or catches. Good soldering is probably the easiest identifiable mark of the experienced jewelry craftsman. Because of the host of variables involved, soldering is the jewelry-making process that demands the most attention and care. And it is the one technique more than any other that is cause for concern for most beginners.

The process requires heat—between 1000° and 2000° F.—which of course means a torch of some kind with controlled focus of this heat.

Torches come in a variety of sizes and powers (heats). From the palm-size Bernz O Matic refillables with a tiny (and not very powerful) pencil-point flame to the still small and common hardware-store tank size. The next notable difference in size is the 20-to-25-pound camper/trailer tanks. These are not very often used by jewelry craftsmen, and this is surprising, for they are convenient, easy to refill, last a long time, and are comparatively inexpensive. Indeed, they will repay their purchase price (approximately twenty to thirty dollars at this writing) in a very short time. The next larger size is the widely used B tank, with acetylene gas. This tank should be equipped with a valve which provides for minor adjustment in its gas dispersal. The valve's use is simply as an indicator of fuel supply and as a check for the on-and-off closing. The value of this torch lies in the ease with which nozzles may be changed; its size

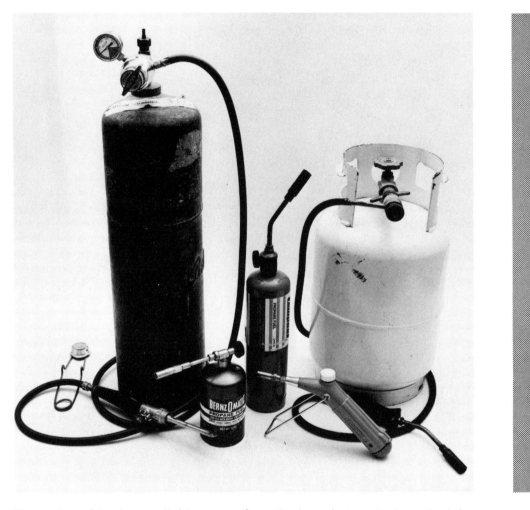

The variety of torches available ranges from the large butane tank on the left to the small hand-held butane refillable on the bottom.

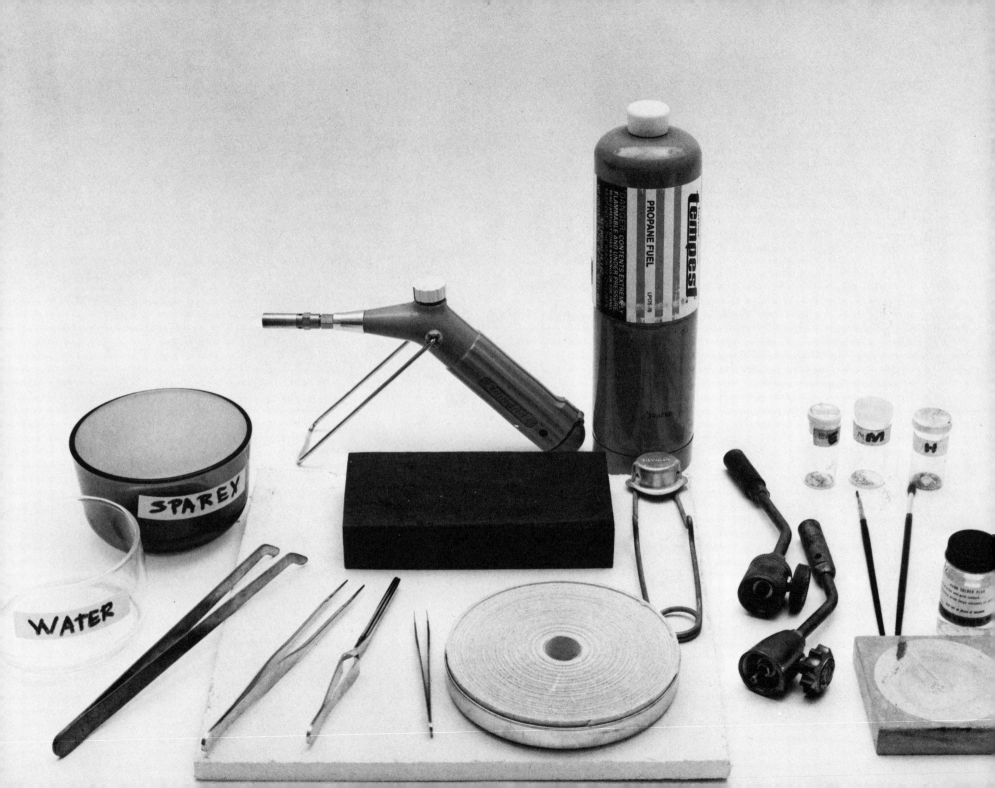

of course; and it is a somewhat hotter flame. The nozzle tips are numbered 1 through 5. And the extremes are not very practically useful. Number 2 works fine for most solderings, number 3 for large pieces, and numbers 4 and 5 for strong, hot flames for melting metal for castings and the like.

One other torch size should be mentioned, and that is the very large combination oxyacetyline torch used by welders. While it may be used with small nozzles for jewelry, it is bulky and expensive—more so than is necessary for jewelry work. But it can be used—like a broom to swat flies.

Soldering also requires some supporting surface for the pieces to be soldered. This can be a charcoal block, an asbestos pad, a ball of support wire, or a pan with pumice granules. Before a charcoal block is employed for soldering, it is a wise practice to wrap its sides with binding wire. This helps to keep the block from splitting, or from separating if it does split. From time to time it is possible to smooth the surface of the block by scraping with a rasp or heavy file—for the block will develop depressions, making it difficult to solder flat work. In addition to the solder itself, hard silver solder flux must be used. The purpose of the flux is to keep the surface to be soldered free of oxidation when heat is applied. It may also be thought of (although this is not strictly speaking true) as a cleaning agent for the metal. Flux may come in paste or liquid form. The author prefers the liquid because it allows the solder bits to be seen. A container is required for the flux—typically a borax slate —and a small brush to apply flux and bits of solder. Although not absolutely essential to the process, it is also wise to include a chemical cleaner. This may be diluted sulfuric acid, or the now more widely used and safer Sparex. This chemical is used before soldering to clean the metal and often after soldering to wash scale and encrusted flux.

The amount, the grade of solder, and the intensity (or really, application) of heat are the variables in soldering. Solder is available in sheet (26 to 28 gauge) or wire (15 to 24 gauge) form, and in five grades, although the middle three are the most widely used. The grades of solder simply mean that

The bits of solder are poured into the flux—in this case medium-grade—for the back piece has yet to be soldered in place.

zinc or brass has been added to allow the solder to flow at predetermined and known temperatures and rate of flow.

Silver (pure melts at	1761° F.
Sterling melts at	1641° F.
I.T. solder flows at	1450°–1550° F.
Hard solder flows at	1425°–1450° F.
Medium solder flows at	1325°–1400° F.
Easy solder flows at	1250°–1325° F.
E-Z Flow solder flows at	1175° F.

As can be seen, excepting the lowest, E-Z Flow (which is used largely for setting catches and pins), the temperature difference between grades averages about 50 degrees. The reason is both simple and direct: The construction of most pieces requires a number of solderings and a craftsman wants to be sure that as he solders he doesn't undo those already done. To prevent this he uses solder which melts at successively lower temperatures. When cutting solder, the bits should resemble large grains of salt. The cut solder bits should be dropped into a pool of flux in the borax slate container before using.

When using more than one grade of solder at a single session, be sure you keep the grades (and the bits) separated. This is done, obviously, by using two or three separate borax slates containing flux and the solder. Another way, if not as immediately obvious— and a trick the author uses—is to use wire for one grade and sheet for the other, when using two. Then both wire (for example, easy) and the medium (in sheet) are dropped into one flux slate. They are then separated as they are used, and easily identified.

It is imperative that the pieces to be joined fit together snugly. Soldering does not fill gaps. This fit should be so tight that no light is visible between the edges or surfaces to be joined. Any line visible before will be visible after soldering. When the joint is fitted tightly, then the brush is used to coat the surface with the silver solder flux and bits of solder are picked up, placed along the edge (spaced about one-eighth of an inch apart). The piece is then heated

Then with a small brush, the bits are placed on the piece.

The brush is used to position the bits.

slowly, to evaporate the flux. This shouldn't be forced, for too much heat too quickly is liable to boil the flux and "spit" the solder off. When the piece is heated, a film of flux may be observed. The heat is continued, and directed to the piece and *not the solder*. The intent is to heat the piece, which in turn will melt the solder. This may mean directing heat to the larger of two pieces. When the metal becomes hot enough, it will cause the solder to flow. Solder wants to flow to the hottest part of the metals, so the craftsman should constantly move his torch about the work. Do not focus on any one spot. As soon as the solder flows, remove the heat. The piece is dropped into the "pickle" (Sparex), removed with copper or wooden tongs, washed with water, and finished. Or the piece is made ready for the next soldering job.

Some soldering hints: When soldering a bezel to a base, place the solder on the inside—if the bezel is to be left with metal around the base. Put the solder on the outside, however, if the metal base is to be cut flush after soldering. In this latter case, another hint involves a cutting procedure: Cut a small piece of wood which will fit within the bezel but be higher. This allows the bezel to be held firmly in a clamp or vise and not deform the bezel.

Wrapping the elements to be soldered with binding wire—as many craftsmen and books recommend— is often more time-consuming and trouble than it is worth. Try to avoid wrapping pieces—and do so only if it is absolutely necessary. For soldering on an awkward form, do not forget to make use of the fine-granuled Carborundum pan for support. And finally, whenever possible, "gang up" on the solderings. It is possible to do two or three solderings at one time, or even a whole series if they are carefully placed.

Heat is applied to the piece overall—not concentrating in any one area. When combining larger pieces, the heat is applied to the larger parts more than the rest.

setting stones

As much as good soldering is a level of craft achievement sought by most beginners as a hallmark of accomplishment, setting a stone well identifies the truly experienced craftsman. Setting a stone incorporates almost all of the basic skills, and in a series, each of which alone stands in strong evidence of craft ability. One must measure, mark, fit, cut, and file with precision. When this has been done, then much of the process is repeated again on a base. The base in turn must be cut and fitted carefully. When all of this has been done, then and only then is the piece—cleaned, filed, polished—ready to have the stone set. And of course, it follows that this too must be done very carefully. Little wonder that there is pride to be derived from completing a stone setting. The incorporation of a gemstone, set well in an attractive piece, lifts the piece from accomplished craft to the realm of fine jewelry.

In setting a stone there are two principal (and very functional) considerations. First, it must be supported. That is to say, it must somehow rest on, or be held up by, something. Second, it must be contained in a given place and not shift. So then, a stone must be both supported and held. These two concerns may be met in a number of ways.

First, the supports. In general, supports fall into three kinds of groupings. One is the flat-table support—or simply a flat piece of metal; obviously, here the stone may slide in any direction. The second is a minor variation of this and provides an incidental groove for a (usually faceted) stone; the stone may still slide, but not as easily. The third kind of support verges onto the holding of a stone setting;

in this support a pronglike base may rise to the sides, designed to allow light to pass through the stone.

The second major consideration in a stone setting is called the "holding" (sometimes also called a "shoulder"). This is for the side of the stone. Holding may be accomplished in two general ways. One is a continuous band of metal which wraps around the stone. Called a "gallery wire," it makes a bezel. And it is usually of fine silver (and very soft). The second kind of holding for a stone is the familiar prong setting. This and the prong base are very close in appearance and often simple in function.

Of the two kinds of holds, the bezel is probably the easier to make and surely the most secure for a stone. Gallery wire may be purchased in a variety of forms ranging from simple flat strips to those with inside shoulder supports. The wire itself is available both plain and decorated.

The gallery wire is wound about the stone tightly, measured for cutting, the stone is of course removed, and then the ends are soldered. The winding may be done in any way convenient—by pushing with pliers (but be careful not to pinch the soft metal and leave marks difficult to remove later), or formed around a ring mandrel. The stone should fit into this loop of metal snugly. This is important. If it is not tight, then you must redo it. When one is sure the stone will fit within the bezel loop, it is then removed and *not touched again*—until the final setting. The temptation to "just check again" may set the stone prematurely—and a host of problems follow. After the stone is removed, the bezel is positioned onto a base and soldered.

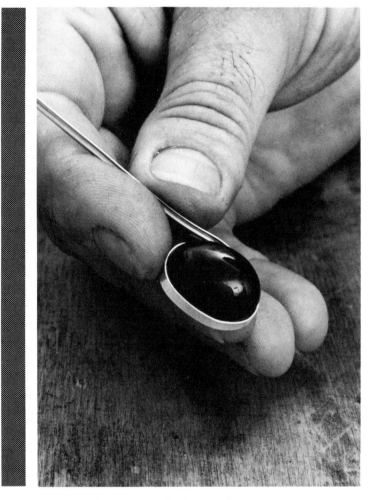

Commercial gallery wire has an inside edge, or shoulder, on which the stone should rest as the wire is wrapped tightly around the stone. The wire length is then cut to fit.

When the edges are tight, the ends are soldered.

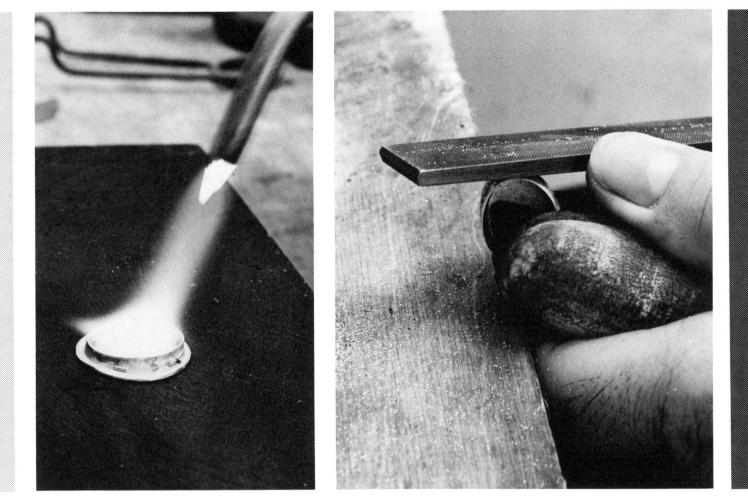

The band is then placed on a base and soldered to the base.

Then the excess silver on the base is cut and filed clean.

The gallery bezel band is then soldered to the piece—in this case a ring.

Then the stone is fitted into place, and carefully secured by the gallery wire being "pushed" into place.

A word about the solderings: Because the bezel fitting and then soldering is usually one operation, with the fitting to base another, "medium" solder should be used for the gallery wire, then one that is "easy" for the fit to base. It is possible to undertake the fitting, the soldering of the gallery-wire ends, and in turn the soldering of the base in one operation, but this is tricky and not recommended for the beginner.

The piece is then finished, polished, and indeed antiqued—and is ready for the stone setting. At this point, a couple of craft tricks are worth mentioning. One is to set the stone to bezel by holding the piece to the top of the stone (in effect, placing the stone in from the bottom). This technique allows for some movement of the stone—with gravity holding it away from the bezel. The second trick is to adhere a piece of sticky wax for grip on top of the stone (stones usually are slippery and can slip into the wrong place easily). The stone should feel as though it is snapping into place. Indeed, it may even make a snapping sound as it fits within the gallery-wire ring.

The next step is the careful pushing of metal to stone for a permanent and tight fit. When the stone is set in place, the metal around the stone is pushed toward the stone. This is done with a "stone pusher" —although any smooth tool will work. Just be sure it is smooth and slightly rounded, so not to scratch the metal. Pushing should be done carefully and by stages. To begin, push at one point; then push the metal from the opposite point. Imagine the stone is a clock face, and if the first push is at 12, the second takes place at 6, the third at 3, and the fourth at 9— and so on. The last step is to rub the metal pusher around the bezel edge, smoothing out any incidental imperfections.

The finished ring with stone set.

63

fastenings

Important in the plans and construction of any piece of jewelry is the directly functional design concern: How is it to be worn? Is it to be hung or pinned; should it be worn loose or held in place tightly? Should its clasps or hooks be hidden or obvious, or, indeed, become part of the design? The term used to describe the array of fastenings that a jewelry craftsman may use is "findings." This covers pins, loops, rings, catches, ear wires, cuff-link backs, springs, snaps, locks, etc. Whatever type of finding is used, it must relate to the purpose and design of the piece in a directly functional way. A pin that doesn't hold is a piece of jewelry that cannot be worn—or if it is worn, may be lost.

Many craftsmen take advantage of commercial findings because they are convenient and, in some instances, entail features impossible to duplicate without specialized manufacturing equipment. This doesn't preclude the jewelry craftsman from handcrafting many of his own findings. A few of the more significant of these findings are shown on page 65 and explained below.

The most basic finding is the simple ring or loop from which a piece (pendant) is hung. Yet even this seemingly simple item must be designed to "fit" the piece. It must be the right size and, if seen, it must be a design form that directly complements or relates to the piece. The loop must be centered properly and allow cord or chain to pass through it easily. Many pieces of jewelry require a ring or loop of metal to hold them. Making rings is a relatively simple undertaking. Wire is wrapped tightly around a nail or a small mandrel or, indeed, anything round (or oval, if that shape is desired) and strong enough to take a tight wrap. This is then secured in a vise and, using the jeweler's saw, cut across the wrapped wire rings. Some craftsmen slide the wrapped wire off the support before cutting (and a few also cut from the inside).

Perhaps the most widely used fastening is the rivet, or post. The post may be employed to join two pieces together loosely. This fastening is done by soldering a piece of wire to a backing or base. The wire is then fitted through a loose slot (one end, of course, with the cap). The other end is then soldered with a cap. The result, in effect, is a kind of small, smooth nut and bolt.

Another widely used finding is the pin back. This consists really of three parts: (1) the hinge, (2) the catch, and (3) the stem (which is available with or without rivet). The hinge and catch are soldered to the back of the jewelry item, and the stem is added after the piece is completed. A couple of considerations are important, beginning with the stem length and placement (direction): Generally, the catch and hinge are spaced as far apart as possible to provide the greatest stability for the piece. This length may be determined by a casual measure of the stem length. A stem too long can easily be cut, filed to a point, and used.

For most uses, the hinge and catch are placed directly horizontal or directly vertical on a pin. When used in the vertical placement, the hinge should be positioned on top. When pin backs are used horizontally, the catch is positioned with its opening facing down (should the catch come open there is the chance and hope it will hold in place). A simple method for finding the center is to place a piece of wire below the piece and try to balance it. However, it may be desirable to place the stem above the middle when it is to be set horizontally—to prevent the piece from falling forward when worn.

To solder hinge and catch, give the base of each a quick pass with a needle file and place a drop of flux on the spots on which the hinge and catch are to be placed. Position both—and then "eyeball" them to be sure that they are aligned properly. Be sure the stem will fit and will close at the right angle when the hinge and catch are soldered. Then place some solder bits in place and solder. Because each is so much smaller than the piece on which it is being soldered, be careful, for the piece is very likely to "pull" heat. If this happens, the catch and hinge will heat more rapidly and cause the solder to run to them.

When hinge and catch have been soldered in place, the stem may be added. Stems with rivets are simply positioned between the hinge openings, and hinge and stem squeezed shut with pliers. Stems without rivets require that a rivet be fitted through its opening and then tapped closed.

Ear supports come in three basic configurations: wire for pierced ears, screw closures for unpierced ears, and a spring clip or folding device, also for unpierced ears. All three types can be found with or without loops, stems, or screw additions for easy attachment of the crafted item. These additions are located on the front, bottom, or side of the finding. In addition, ear findings are available with incidental "design" elements such as small domes or a ball, or an unusually wide, flat surface. When working with unadorned earring findings to which design elements are to be added, it is wise to open the finding for convenience. Be sure, if the finding is the spring type, the spring is removed before adding heat.

Other kinds of fastenings include a vast array of loops, rings, catches, hooks, and whatnot. Only a few of the more popular and commercial items are shown here.

The extent to which a finding can be made depends only on the versatility of the jewelry designer. It is probably a wise practice to begin using commercial findings before attempting to make your own. But by all means, at some point early in your jewelry making, do design and make an individualized fastening.

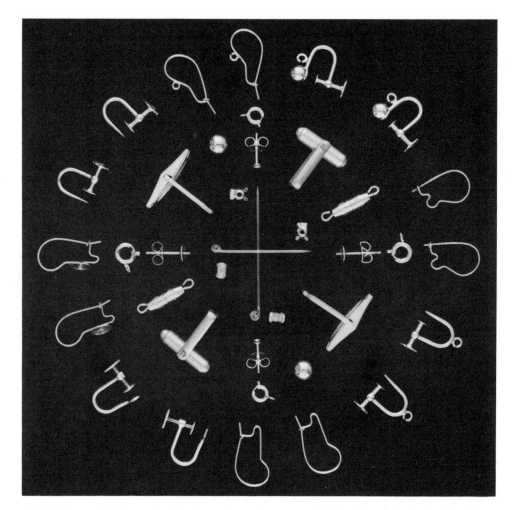

A selection of the tremendous number of commercial findings (or fastenings) available to the jeweler: earrings, jump rings, cuff links, pin backs, etc. Even silver balls.

finishing (polishing)

Finishing is the rather broad term used here to describe the "polishing" process. However, the process begins in fact well before a piece reaches the polishing wheel. Finishing requires a piece of metal to progress from rough edge and surface through a series of stages to a degree of polish. Many craftsmen prefer not to have their work highly polished, but this doesn't mean that the surface is not very smooth, or a small step away from being glossy. Finishing also includes techniques such as antiquing, brush finish, or punching and texturing the surface.

Basically, finishing entails the use of files, assorted "cutting" papers, "cutting" compounds on a buffing wheel, and final polishing. The three major steps—(1) files, (2) cutting papers, and (3) cutting compounds—overlap each other slightly. A medium-rough file, for example, may in fact be smoother than a very rough paper.

When a piece is to be filed, do not begin with too rough a cut. It may be possible to skip a cut and proceed with a finer file. Working from rough to fine cut should also mean the craftsman works from heavy (rough) pressure to easy (fine) pressure and with the last strokes very light—almost wipes. When the piece has an almost sheenlike surface of imperceptible file scratches, then it may be "papered."

The most common paper used by jewelers is emery. This is available in numbers ranging from number 3 rough to number 4/0, which is very fine. The stages in between are not unlike the numbering system used for saw blades: from number 3 rough, to numbers 2, 1, 0, 2/0, 3/0, and 4/0. (Also note that emery cloth [not paper] may be used and it is specified in grit numbers: number 160 is considered rough, number 220 is a medium grit, number 420 is a very fine grit, and number 600 is considered a "polishing" cloth. The cloth is stronger than the paper, and correspondingly more expensive, but it is also considerably more durable. Unlike paper, the cloth can be torn into small pieces for working in corners, and with no fear that the cloth will disintegrate.)

Do not begin with too rough a paper. For most work with paper, it helps to have it glued or stapled to a backing of wood (or even a dowel form for convenience). The intent, of course, is to reduce the size and depth of scratches by making smaller ones. Successive strokes with the paper are always at different angles. Do not stop working with the paper too soon in the finishing process. It is a mistake to use the next stage in order to buff out marks. Buffing will merely polish the scratches.

But before turning to the polishing wheel, another stage in the finishing process often takes place at this juncture. This is called antiquing, or blackening. Silver, if not rubbed or polished occasionally, will in time darken, or oxidize. This is particularly evident on the insides of forms, or on protected parts which do not receive any minor rubbing action. This darkening is not always even, nor will the area blacken thoroughly. To effect and control this blackening action the jewelry craftsman can make areas he wants black, as he wishes. To do this he uses liver of sulfur (there are others, but this is by far the most widely used). This is popularly known as antiquing.

To effect this blackening of the surface, the piece is heated lightly (too hot to handle by hand, but not so hot that it is annealed), and then dipped into a container of liver of sulfur. The piece may, of course, have the solution brushed on, although this very often requires two or three brushings, since the heat in the piece dissipates. For this reason the complete one-step immersion is preferred. But if this is not possible (size of piece, or shape, or desire for control of the antiquing), the piece must then be reheated during the process.

Liver of sulfur is available commercially in 1-pound and 5-pound containers, and comes in chunk form. It is a dark yellow ocher in color, and smells like rotten eggs. And the color and smell are a clue to its condition. The absence of color or smell reveals a weak, or unusable, compound. To mix the solution, a chunk about the size of a tablespoon is stirred into about two cups of hot water. The chunk dissolves, and the solution has a dark brown hue to it. Both the mixed solution and the original chunk pieces should be kept covered and out of light to save their potency.

The buffing (polishing) wheel employs high speed to do quickly what formerly took many hours of tedious hand labor. A buffing wheel is simply a motorized unit that turns a shaft or spindle (tapered shaft) with wheels (buffs) of various materials to which have been applied abrasive or polishing compounds. Buffs are constructed of different materials and are available in different sizes, thicknesses, and shapes. In general, they come in two broad categories: cutting buffs and "coloring" (the term for polishing) buffs.

Cutting buffs, in turn, may be thought of as hav-

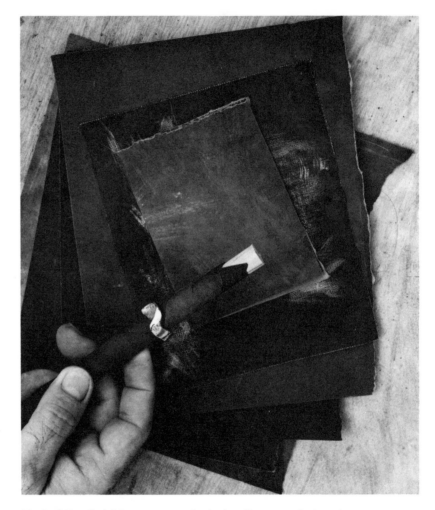

Part of the finishing process includes the use of abrasive (and polishing) papers and cloths. A few of these are shown with paper wrapped around a dowel for work on the inside of rings.

ing two cutting actions: coarse and medium. Coarse cutting buffs are designed to be used with pumice or Lea Compound or emery. The buff material is likely to be leather or heavy muslin. Another cutting-tool compound is really a tool; this is what is called a "bright boy." It is a rubber disk that has been impregnated with cutting compound—but although it cuts well without adding other compounds, many craftsmen (the author included) add some tripoli. And then use it sparingly. A bright boy can almost be considered a shaping tool not unlike a fine tool. It is easily the quickest cutting action this side of a file. Medium cutting buffs are used with tripoli as a rule and would be made from muslin or felt to retain edges. Polishing buffs are used with jeweler's rouge, and are usually of soft flannel; but felt may also be used here again.

It is very important to label all buffs and use only the compound on the wheel. Under no circumstance should compounds be mixed. If they are mixed, then obviously the cutting-polishing action is altered. For this reason it is important to wash all traces of compound from a piece before turning to another. Cleaning the compound grease is done with a mixture of ammonia and soap and water (the more ammonia the quicker the washing, and the quicker one's eyes water). Let the piece sit a few minutes in the ammonia wash, and then brush with a soft rag or an old brush (a toothbrush works fine). Dry the piece off and continue working on the wheel.

Working with cutting buffs, one can begin with Lea Compound, which cuts very fast. However, as with the use of files, do not feel obliged to begin with this compound. It is possible your piece can start with the

The silver being polished is held by the fingers at the top, and is held to the buffing wheel at the near bottom quarter of the wheel.

next level of cutting action, which is tripoli. Most craftsmen, in fact, begin with this action. If scratches are still discernible, then wash and go back to the Lea.

The final stage is the polishing with the jeweler's rouge. And it is this compound that imparts a high gloss to silver. Rouge comes in different colors, with red the most popular for work with sterling. If scratches still appear, then the piece has not been properly buffed before it was polished. And the only solution is to return to a cutting-action buff.

To work on the buffing wheel one should observe a few obvious cautions, and a few not so obvious.

First, be sure your hair is tied and not liable to be caught in the spinning spindle. The same caution holds true for loose clothing. Wear clothing that you can afford to get dirty—and with rouge it will seem to sift through the pores of the cloth. Eyeglasses are not absolutely necessary, but are helpful if you have them.

Second, be sure the buff is properly and securely attached to the spindle. And third, hold the piece properly.

It could take a volume alone to explain how to work with a buffing wheel, but a few rudimentary approaches ought to suffice. Hold the piece by the top, with your fingers over the top edge. This prevents the top edge from being caught and pulling the piece into the machine. In effect, the wheel must run off the piece. Be careful about holding a piece with a ring clamp or some other tool: It hides the friction heat, and it is possible to buff your piece away. Chains and small items should be held firmly and backed on a piece of scrap wood. And finally, read the manufacturer's instructions as to the proper wheels for different compounds. In general, try to work with a hard-edged wheel for cutting (to retain the edge on your work), and keep to the shape of the work being buffed.

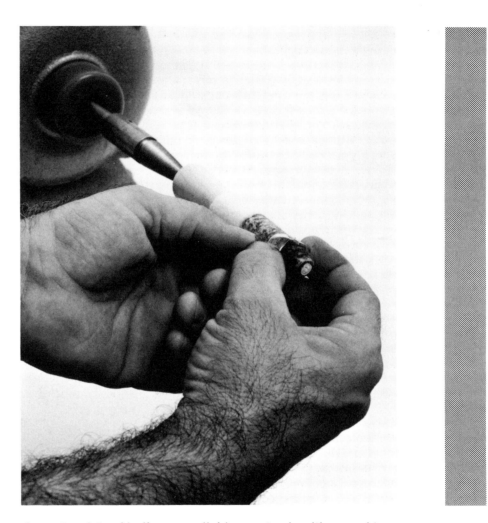

A great variety of buffs are available—not only with regard to material but also shape. Here a ring buff is being used for work on the inside of a ring.

casting

Casting is a process by which molten metal is poured, or flung, into the opening or cavity of a mold.

Casting sterling silver requires: (1) the silver, which may be in the form of granules, although scrap pieces of sheet and wire work adequately, (2) a torch capable of reaching more than 1800° F. heat in order to melt the metal, and (3) a cavity, which is the opening or hole into which the molten metal is poured. Very simple cavities can be made by cutting into the surface of a charcoal block. These crude cuts result likewise in crude castings. These are little more than hunks of rough-formed metal which require a good deal of finishing.

Beyond its quaint nostalgia, or for demonstration purposes, cuttlebone (simply a heat-resistant fishbone) casting is rarely done. However, it does allow for some detail, provided the model has no undercuts. Because the bone is so soft, it is possible to actually push impressions into the marrow. The sides can be forced together over a hard model, and by squeezing the model you can "crush" the bone into making the impression. After the model is removed, flow channels are cut from the cavity to the edge of the bone. The bone sides are secured with binding wire and molten metal is poured down the flow channels into the cavity.

More elaborate, slightly more expensive, but much easier to undertake and far more convenient, is "lost wax" casting. This process entails the need for two additionally important pieces of equipment. One of these is the centrifugal casting machine and the second is a small burn-out kiln (simply a high-temperature oven). The process also entails a casting flask and a pair of long-handled tongs. The flask mentioned is a steel tube 2 to 3 inches in diameter and some 2 to 6 inches in length, much the same size as a small soup can.

Now to the specifics of the process: There are five distinct steps and each is covered in detail below. The five steps are: (1) making the model, (2) setting

Just a few of the great variety of waxes available in sheet, block, and wire form with a tube blank for rings.

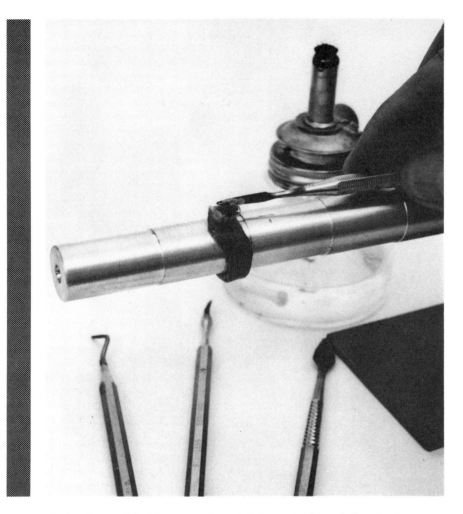

A ring is modeled in wax using stainless-steel modeling tools, which are heated on a candle—or in this case an alcohol lamp.

it in the flask and mixing and pouring the investment, (3) the burn-out of the model in the kiln, (4) melting the metal and releasing the spring-wound centrifugal caster, and (5) the retrieval and finishing of the cast item.

The first step is making the model. Although the model is usually of wax (hence the "lost wax" process), it should be noted that any combustible material will work: bugs, leaves, pine cones, plastic buttons. . . . The waxes used by craftsmen are not like the typical table candle. Some are derived from natural sources and some are synthetic, derived from petroleum or minerals. The waxes may be very hard or very soft (though natural or synthetic is not a clue here); they may be very brittle or very sticky. Each needs to be worked in its own way. Soft waxes are impractical, if not impossible, to carve. They must be formed and shaped by pressure and heat. Hard wax, on the other hand, is virtually impossible to mold in this fashion and must be carved, cut, drilled, or filed. Some waxes are designed to adhere different grades of wax together and others to be melted in order to cast a replica. In the latter instance, the wax is melted and poured—to make a model to cast. Wax may be ordered in a variety of forms: sheets, slabs, cubes, and all shapes and thickness of wire. It may even be ordered in rough blank forms—which, however, few craftsmen use.

The tools used with wax may range from flattened nails, to tools specifically designed for wax work, to electrically heated spatulas. Heating the tools helps in forming, and this may be done over a simple candle flame or over an alcohol-lamp-cleaner flame or even in a dish of hot water. There is no single technique for working with wax. Wax can be melted on, melted off, scraped off, joined in parts—indeed, any way one works is acceptable. But remember that casting does not correct flaws. The more finished the model, the easier it is to complete the piece when cast. One final point: Do not make the model too

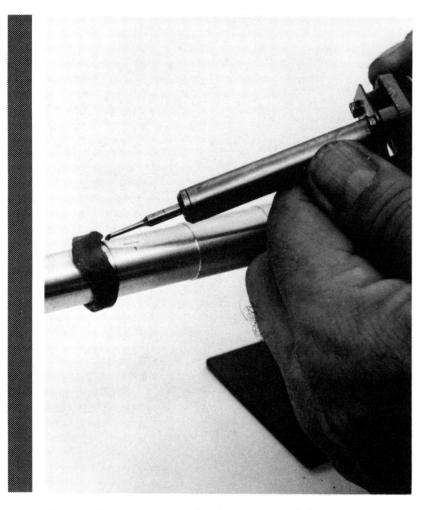

Also available is an electrically heated modeling tool.

heavy. It will appear fragile and feel light in wax, but becomes both durable and heavy when cast in silver. Indeed, it will become approximately ten times heavier.

The second major step in the process is setting the model in the base and flask. The base is a ring of rubber or aluminum. Rubber is by far the better base, for it makes a tight seal when the flask is attached to the base prior to pouring. The base has a slight center mound which helps to raise the model and creates a funnellike form when the base is removed later. The casting flask is a heavy steel tube (open at both ends) which holds the investment and will not deform in the "burn-out" kiln. It fits within the arm of the casting machine next to the crucible. The model is held in position before investing by wax wires called "sprues." Attach the wax sprues so that they join the model to the center of the base mound.

When burned out along with the model, the cavities left by the sprues will serve as channels for the molten metal during the casting. The model should be set so that no part of it is closer than three-eighths of an inch from the sides and top of the flask. Because the sprues serve as flow channels, their direction and angle should be as straight and smooth as possible from mound to model. No parts of the sprues or model should cause the metal to flow "backward." The metal wants to flow easily and quickly, and should be allowed to do so.

When the model is positioned, the steel casting flask is set on the base ready for investment, the substance which will harden to become the actual mold. Casting investment is available as a very dry powdery substance and commonly purchased at craft-supply houses. It contains cristobalite, silica, gypsum, and assorted compounds in smaller measure. Cristobalite, the major ingredient, is a form of silica, but one which allows for slight expansion and contraction. Silica is a refractory material (not altered by heat). And gypsum is a form of plaster of paris

The finished wax model is then set on the rubber base, using wax "sprues." The model is set to allow for the easy flow of silver into the cavity.

The model should not be set any closer than one-quarter to three-eighths of an inch from the sides and top of the flask.

and serves to hold the investment components together. The other components include carbon and some copper sulfite. Investment is mixed much like plaster of paris, although the 40 to 45 percent ration of water to mix is more critical. A simple, direct, and reasonably reliable method of determining this ratio results from filling the flask (with model in place) *almost* to the top with water. The model, of course, displaces water (and the larger the model, the less water and therefore less mix). If in doubt, however, mix a bit extra. The water is then poured into a mixing bowl and stirred until the investment is of a light creamy consistency. Do not mix vigorously, for it is important not to stir in air pockets. Once the mixing has begun, stirring and pouring should be completed within ten minutes. The mixed investment is poured. Do not stint on the pouring—overflow if necessary. The flask is then rapped sharply with a hard tool to dislodge any surface-tension bubbles that may adhere to the model. The bubbles leave tiny metal nodules on the cast piece if not dislodged. A solution called "de-bubble-izer" is sometimes painted on the model in order to break this surface tension. Many professional-level craftsmen use a vacuum bell to draw air to the surface of the flask and a vibrator to shake the investment.

The invested flask is then left to harden. The time this takes depends on the size of the flask, the humidity, and the mix proportions. Generally, hardening takes about half an hour. After the investment has solidified, the base may be removed. The hard but still damp investment flask must be left to "cure" for at least an hour. Three or four hours are better, and leaving it overnight is not unreasonable. On the other hand, the flask should not be left so long that it dries out. A completely dry flask is liable to crack in the burn-out, and, at best, gives a poor casting.

The next step is the burn-out. This is undertaken in a small kiln which is a heavy-walled high-heat oven, capable of temperatures of 2000° F. The best burn-out kilns have vents for the escape of moisture and fumes, and may have an attached pyrometer.

The investment is mixed with a spatula in a rubber bowl. The mix should be of a thick, creamy consistency.

The mixed investment is then poured carefully into the flask. This should come to the top—and overflow, if necessary.

When the mix is hard, the base is removed from the flask, revealing the conical pour hole.

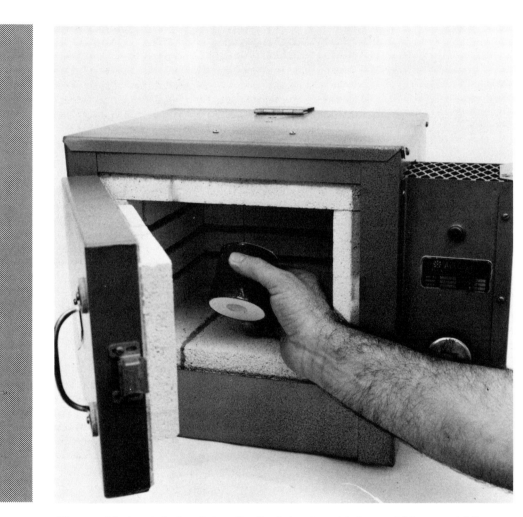

Thoroughly hard, but not dry, the flask is placed into a cold burn-out kiln. The flask is placed with the pour hole down. The kiln is then, of course, turned on.

However, a small enameling kiln works suitably if the doors are left ajar. The most convenient-size kiln for the home craftsman measures about a cubic foot, with an inside measure of 4 to 6 cubic inches.

The flask, with the base now removed, is placed on supports in the kiln with hole end down, to allow the wax to melt out. The temperature of the kiln is then raised slowly because it is necessary (1) to dry out the remaining moisture (heating too fast creates steam, which will burst the flask mold), (2) to melt the wax, and (3) to evaporate carbons in the flask. One way of calculating the necessary 1300° F. is by placing a small piece of aluminum wire in the kiln—because this melts at 1300°. Maximum temperature should be reached in about an hour for small flasks and about two to two and a half hours for large flasks. The flask should be checked by removing with long-handled tongs and viewing the bottom openings. Openings should be clean and white—free of any tracings of gray or black carbon. When the flask is clean, the temperature may then be reduced. The most desirable flask temperature for casting is around 800°. Estimating this, of course, is not easy. Another direct and simple way of working in the absence of temperature certainty is to undertake the following steps without haste and in steady and unhurried moves. By the time the flask is removed and set on its side in the casting machine, the silver is melted, and the arm is ready to be released, then the flask temperature has reduced sufficiently. The reason for this drop is to have the flask hot enough to hold the metal fluid in the pour, but not so hot that the metal cannot solidify once it is in the mold.

The centrifugal caster is a spring-wound machine with an arm of some 12 to 14 inches centered on top of the enclosed spring base. One end of the arm holds the crucible, with the flask facing the crucible. The other end holds counterbalancing weights. These

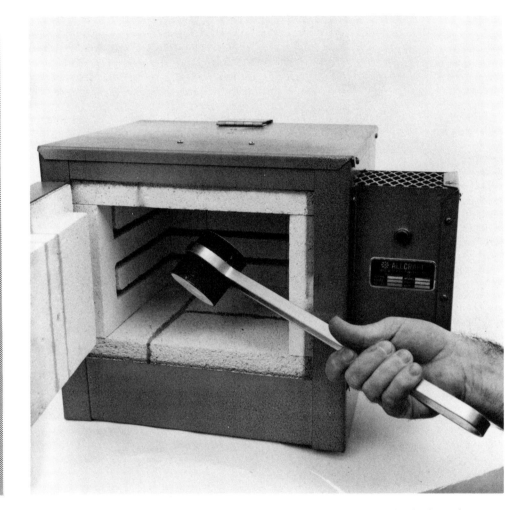

The flask is then brought to temperature to burn out all wax. And when the bottom opening is free of any traces of carbon it may be removed in preparation for casting. It is then handled with long-handled tongs and placed into the casting-machine support.

may be set by following manufacturer's directions. Although they are supposed to be set for each casting, in practice once they are set they are usually left alone. The machine also has a heavy pin in the base which is raised after the arm is wound in order to hold the spring-tensioned arm. The pin prevents the arm from unwinding until ready. The casting machine should be set securely in a protective shield. This could be a metal trash can. Do not wind the spring (and arm) too tightly. An easy one or two turns are all that is necessary. The centrifugal force of an ounce of silver is strong—do not spring the machine too tightly.

The crucible/flask end of the arm is horizontally hinged to allow the arm a right-turn bend. This allows the silver in the crucible to be flung into the flask opening—rather than being left to one side when the machine spins. Metal is placed in the crucible and melted by torch. As it is being melted, it is helpful to add some powdered borax to prevent air from oxidizing on the surface. When the silver is liquid-looking and glistening in appearance, the arm is held (the retaining pin drops), the torch is removed, and the arm is released simultaneously. It swings vigorously and the liquid metal is centrifugally flung from the crucible into the flask. The arm continues to revolve for a dozen or more turns. When it comes to a complete stop, the tongs are used to lift the flask (with its red-hot core) and it is then dunked into a container of water. The thermal change and the water break down the investment and free the metal cast. The (rough-looking) result can then be sawn free of the (now) metal sprues and the bottom plug. The plug, of course, stems from the conical mound in the base. This has served both as a funnel device to direct the metal flow and also as a safety for overflow. The casting is then finished and completed, as desired.

When the metal is melted and obviously liquid, the balance arm may be held —just enough to release the holding pin—the pin drops, and the arm is released. The arm swings rapidly, flinging the molten metal into the flask cavity. The flask with the cast core, still red hot, is gripped with the tongs and taken to the bucket of water. It is then dunked into the water. With a great cloud of steam and rumbling noises, the investment mix "breaks" down and releases the cast item.

The cast item: a ring with base plug of extra metal.

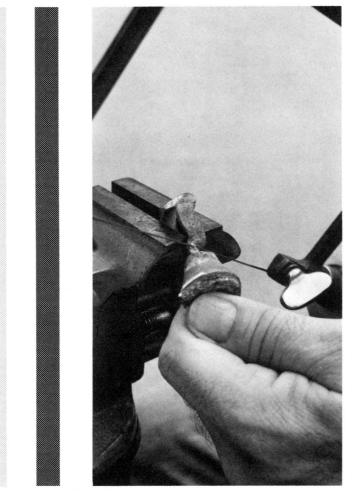

The ring is cut from the base plug.

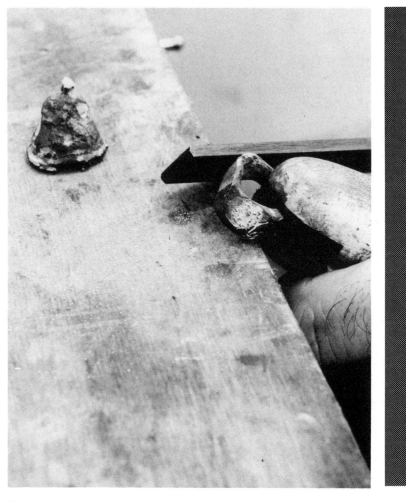

The ring is then filed and finished as usual.

THE DESIGN AND CONSTRUCTION OF A PIECE OF JEWELRY

The following series of photos and sketches illustrates in step-by-step sequence the design and construction of a piece of contemporary jewelry. Beginning with the rough graphic germination of an idea, the piece passes through a number of sketches, notes, and alterations while being produced. During this process the mental picture of the piece is becoming clarified. At this stage the idea may be clear, or it may be very vague in major parts of its structure. Even with a piece that has a number of elements unresolved, the designer may indeed begin, certain of his ability to develop any parts left vague as he proceeds; but though sometimes this happens, very often it does not. A design that cannot be solved during the process should be left to sit until such time as inspiration strikes—or it may end up as chunks of metal for the casting crucible.

It is possible, although not recommended, for the beginner to start with only an abstract intent. The piece is begun with the conviction that the pieces in stages will provide the necessary conceptual stimuli for stages that follow. This is not easy to do; there is an enormously high failure rate. The author prefers to begin with sketches, however rough. And as the idea begins to take form in metal, I modify the piece as necessary. At this stage—or *before* the actual construction begins—it is not unwise to cut and paste paper forms to suggest sheet forms to be cut. Nor is it time wasted to take some soft (aluminum) wire and bend and shape a wire form to correspond to the shape desired. This need not be forged to get the sense of form and size and direction desired.

Let us proceed then through the various stages shown in designing and making the piece illustrated. The piece began with the sketches, or the idea for the piece penned quickly on the back of a napkin. As the drawings suggest, the overall idea was reason-

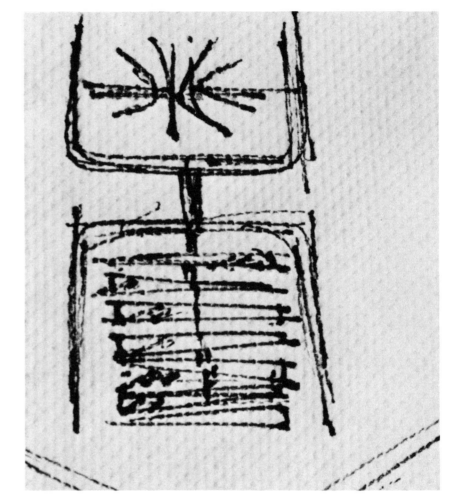

This, and the illustrations on page 84, are sketches of a contemplated piece.

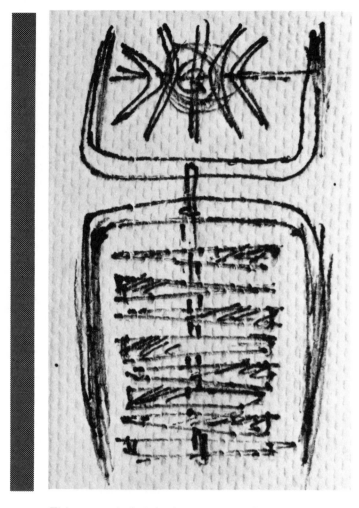

This second sketch shows some minor variation.

Here, an element has been superimposed on the sketch.

ably clear, if the details were not, particularly the specifics of the inside on the top, and the relationship between top and bottom.

The next stage was to determine the gauge of the wire to be used, although this in fact was not a particularly deliberative decision. In this case, 10-gauge square was used for the major elements on top and bottom, and for the elements on the inside of the bottom. Obviously, thinner gauge (12) was intended, and used for the remaining parts: the top cross piece, the top forged pieces, and the vertical support piece on the bottom. The remaining wire was a few short pieces of 12-gauge round for the oval loop between top and bottom, and for the loop (not seen) employed as a slide hold on the backside. The amounts of solder and flux were, of course, negligible.

The next obligation was to cut the lengths of wire to be used to the appropriate length. This was done by sawing—and note, slightly shorter in length than desired for the final formed piece. The reason was simple: The forming process would lengthen—stretch —the wire, and this then would have been longer than the cut piece. How much shorter to cut the pieces is a matter of experience, and like the chef with a recipe: a "pinch" shorter.

The wire was next formed to shape, the ends being flattened first, being sure that each end was the same in shape and formed length. Next, the short pieces for the inside bottom part were formed. These were formed with compound shapes—forged in one direction, then turned and shaped in the opposite-side direction. Hopefully, this change in direction would not be noticeable along the length of the wire. Then the large top and bottom pieces were bent at right angles at each side. The middle was then formed carefully. At some point along the way, the top elements' smaller pieces were formed and shaped. So also the bottom middle support, and the top middle wire, were fashioned. It should be noted that bending the wire can be undertaken in any one of a number of ways, depending on how one wants the finished bend to look: sharp-angled, or soft curve. And of course, through the process the pieces were annealed.

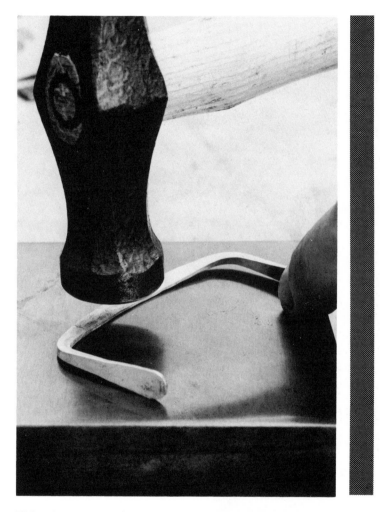

This photo shows forming on the square wire after it has been bent to change direction.

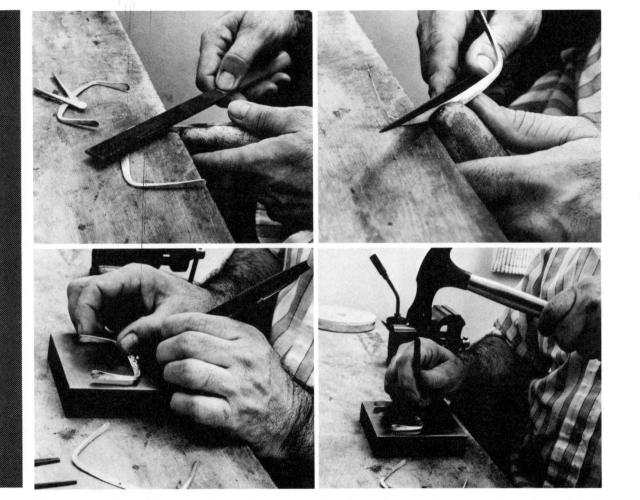

The piece is filed with a large hand file (number-2 cut) on the outside and on the edges. A half-round file is used on the inside curves. With a pen, the spot to be drilled is very carefully marked. A center punch is held on the spot and rapped sharply with a carpenter's hammer.

When the pieces had been formed, they were then filed smooth. The large flat file and the smaller flat needle file were used on the outside curves and on the flat surfaces. A half-round (this could have been a round) file was used on the inside curves.

Next, the top and bottom pieces were marked precisely, for drilling. The marked hole was then tapped with a center punch, using a carpenter's hammer. (This provides a burr edge for the drill, and prevents the bit from "wandering.") The holes were then drilled carefully. (Following the drilling, the backsides may need a light filing to remove the residue of drilled metal.) With all the forming done, and then the drilling, all the elements were ready to be joined together.

A wise practice at this point is to lay out all the pieces, being sure they relate as planned, and that additional pieces need not be formed, or pieces changed in size or shape. In this case, it can be seen how closely the forged pieces did resemble the original sketch. And it should be noted that even at this point it was possible to alter, change, adjust—in virtually any way desired. The intention is not necessarily to "copy" a sketch, but rather to make a good-looking piece of jewelry. It may be that the piece doesn't show certain dimensions in the same manner the sketch does. By all means, rely on the actual elements to make decisions.

The next stage was soldering the pieces together. Basically, the top and bottom were separate structures. With the pieces arranged carefully, it was possible to "gang up" on the soldering. It took a little longer to place the pieces carefully, and place the solder bits even more carefully, without dislodging other solders or the pieces themselves. But when they were in place, the piece was then soldered at one time. When both top and bottom pieces were soldered, an oval ring was fashioned from 12-gauge round wire and put through the hole in top and bottom. This loop was then in turn soldered. At this point, merely because it was convenient, the piece was turned over and a loop made and soldered to make the piece a pendant which could be hung. The piece was now essentially finished.

Next the piece was buffed lightly with tripoli and

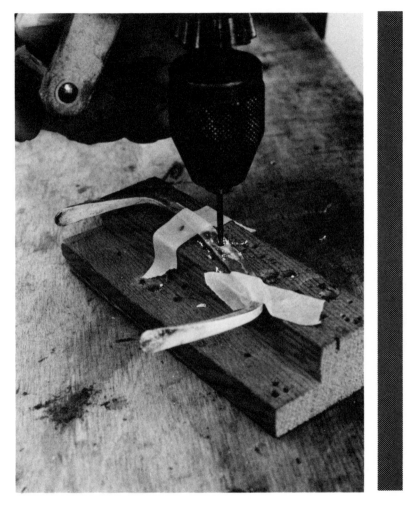

Then, very carefully, the appropriate size drill bit is used (in this case with a hand drill). The piece to be drilled is taped in place to prevent turning. Then the drill handle is turned slowly and a hole is made.

Here are all the formed parts together, ready for positioning and soldering.

The bottom half is soldered—with all the elements placed together and done at once.

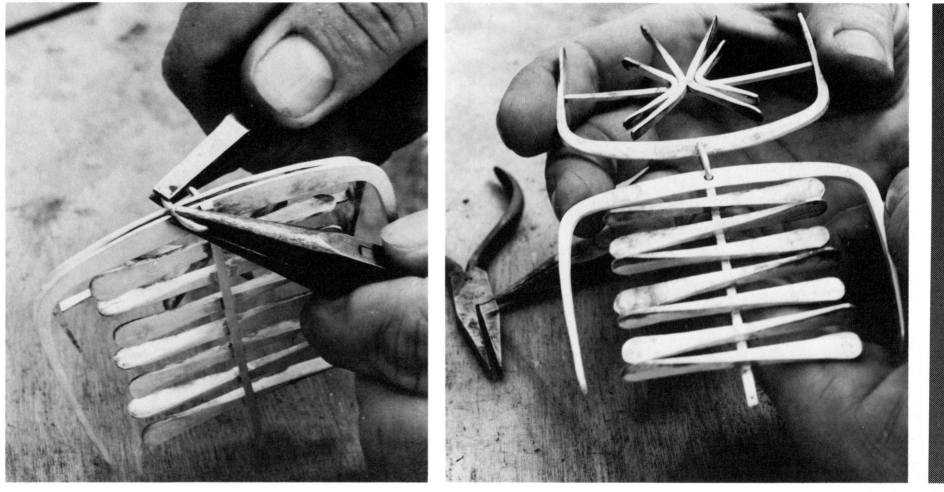

An oval loop of round wire is opened and put through both top and bottom holes and then soldered closed.

The piece is now structurally complete, and ready for finishing.

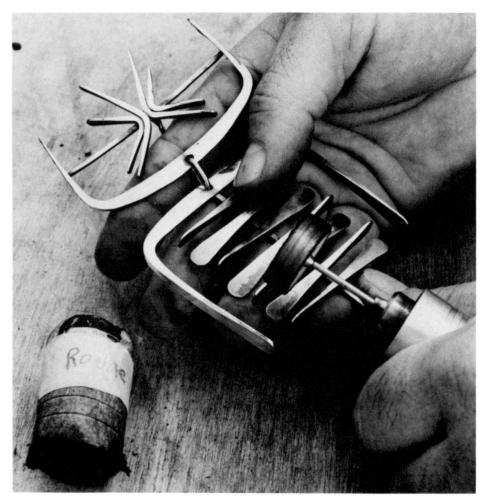

A finishing step includes the application of liver of sulfur (antiquing) before polishing, to contrast in high luster.

The piece is given a final polishing.

then washed with a combination of ammonia, water, and soap, and wiped dry. Following the tripoli buffing, the piece was heated and liver of sulfur brushed over the piece, which blackened it. (This is called antiquing.) Following the application of liver of sulfur, the piece was rubbed lightly with a paste of fine pumice which provided a dull sheen. The pumice is simply a fine granular powder which was dabbed with wet fingers and in turn rubbed on the piece. The final stage was the polishing with jeweler's rouge, using a felt wheel.

The finished piece is close in size and appearance to the original sketch. It must be noted, in all candor, that while these photos were taken dissatisfaction with the top elements grew. The piece was taken apart on the top and those elements were removed. A single vertical forged wire (the same size) was added, and the pieces were then changed in shaped angle, and the whole inside unit resoldered. Indeed, the piece now resembles the original sketch even more.

The time spent on the construction is hard to recall precisely, but would have to approximate three hours. The photographic session for this particular piece began shortly after breakfast and stopped before a late lunch. And this time also includes time for the lighting to be changed; repeat shots were taken, too, and ones in which camera angles were changed. It must also be noted that in practice the actual fabrication might have been done in slightly different ways, had it not been necessary to photograph the making of the piece. For example, I might have put all the solderings together on the face side —top and bottom—and then done them together. But it seemed to make photographic sense to separate this particular process.

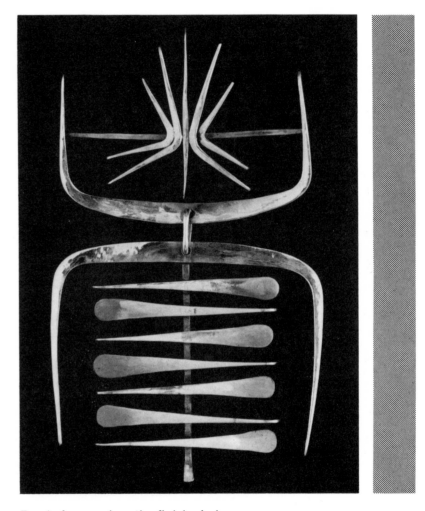

Ready for wearing, the finished piece.

GLOSSARY

Abrasive Any rough tool or material designed to wear away metal surfaces. This includes files, emery paper, and compounds.

Alloy A mixture of metals. Sterling silver is in a sense an alloy, for it includes 75 parts copper to 925 parts silver.

Anneal Annealing is the process by which metal is softened or resoftened after being stiffened, or tempered, by beating and hard bending.

Anvil Typically a heavy metal form on which silver is beaten or forged. For working with silver the anvil surface should be free of dents—and indeed polished.

Asbestos A nonheat-conducting material—very often in the form of a pad placed below the working surface on which one heats.

Beating The broad term often used to describe forging, or when metal is physically altered in form.

Bench pin A piece of wood, usually with a wedge-shape cut on the outer working edge. This is secured to a work surface and becomes a work area itself for cutting, filing, etc.

Bending The broad term used to describe silver when it is changed in direction but not basic shape.

Bezel A strip of pure silver that is designed to fit around a stone for setting.

Buffing The process by which metal is polished—usually by machine, and usually with rouge. It may be done by hand and it need not technically include rouge. Buffs (or the wheels employed) come in a great variety of materials, for very specific purposes.

Butane The fuel (and tank) used in a common torch.

Cabochon Probably the most widely used gemstone shape. It has a flat base and is rounded on top. The stone may be square or rectangular.

Casting The process by which molten metal is formed into a mold.

C-clamp A simple clamp used for fastening—usually a bench pin and shaped as the letter C.

Charcoal Usually in a block—simply burned wood which reflects heat well.

Crucible A small container made of nonrefracting (heat-bearing) material into which molten metal is poured or heated for casting.

Cutting The process by which metal is cut or sawed, or abrased away by "cutting compounds."

Dapping block A square block of steel with various-size (and -depth) cupped depressions. Metal circles are placed within and with dapping tools "punched" to a dome shape.

Draw plate Steel plate with fine holes through which wire may be pulled to decrease its diameter—and doing so increase its length. The metal is pulled with draw tongs.

Ductility That quality in metal that allows it to be pulled or "drawn" without breaking. An ounce of fine silver may be stretched for miles in length.

Emery A popular grade of abrasive which may come in paper, sticks, or as a compound for the "polishing" wheel. It is used to remove scratches and marks from metal.

Files Metal tools with ridges of metal designed to wear away silver. They come in a variety of sizes, forms, and abrasive abilities (cuts).

Findings The term used to cover the variety of catches, loops, pins, and backs by which jewelry is held when worn.

Fire scale A grayish coating of oxidized metal on the surface of silver after it has been heated to a high degree. It is seen only after the metal has been finished (polished).

Flux Liquid or paste, very often of borax, coated on metal prior to soldering. Designed to keep the silver from oxidizing, it also helps the solder flow to the metal surface.

Forging The process by which metal is beaten to alter its shape. Requires hard hammers and a base plate.

Forming A combination of beating (forging) and bending to shape metal. Very often this is done on a forming base of wood or metal stakes.

Gallery wire. Or bezel wire—really a thin strip of metal, and usually of fine silver. Designed to fit around a gemstone for setting.

Gauge The term used to describe a thickness of metal. The Brown & Sharpe circular gauge is one of the standards used. The lower the number, the thicker the metal.

Hammer A metal hammer—hard, and distinct from the softer mallet. Available in different weights and shaped heads for beating or forging metal. "Forging" hammers should be kept polished.

Hardening The common term for the tempering of metal.

Heating As the term implies, the process by which metal is heated. This term may also refer to annealing.

Ivory White material derived from the tusks of elephants, or from whale teeth. Popular in jewelry because it makes a good contrast with silver.

Kiln A small furnace used to burn out wax or materials from an investment prior to casting.

Lapidary The broad term used to describe the process of cutting, shaping, and polishing gemstones.

Lea Compound An abrasive compound which is a fast "cutting" agent.

Liver of sulfur Rough-shape chunks used to oxidize metal— or blacken (antique) it.

Malleability The term used to describe the pliability of metal. It is capable of being pulled, pushed, drawn, etc.

Mallet A "soft" hammer, which may be composed of fiber, rawhide, rubber, plastic, or wood. It is designed for "bending" metal, as distinct from beating.

Mandrel A tapered bar to which buffs are attached on a buffing wheel. Also a metal form tapered to accommodate ring shaping or, in a larger scale, for shaping bracelets.

Melting Reducing metal by heat to a molten state. The melting point of metals is that point at which the metal turns to liquid. The melting point of sterling silver is 1641° F. Lead's, by contrast, is a little over 600°, and platinum's is over 3000°.

Mold A cavity into which molten metal is poured.

Nitric acid A powerful acid which aids in removing fire scale from jewelry. Not for the inexperienced craftsman. It must be handled with great care.

Oxidation The natural action of air and time will blacken silver. To control this, the work is often deliberately blackened by immersing it in a solution of liver of sulfur.

Pickle An acid that "cleans" silver before and after soldering. The most widely used pickle now is Sparex II, which is a safe, commercially available solution. Pickling may also be made from ten parts water and one part sulfuric acid.

This proportion may be altered for faster or slower cleaning action.

Polishing The process by which metal is taken by stages from a rough surface to a high gloss.

Propane A fuel used in torches for heating.

Pumice An abrasive material.

Punch Either a sharp-pointed tool used to mark and start a hole for drilling, or a rounded tool used with a dapping block.

Ring clamp A holding device unique to jewelry, made of three pieces of wood. Two are joined in the middle with a band of metal. The inside ends of each piece are covered in leather. The third piece of wood is a wedge shape which serves to spread the two pieces and tightens one end.

Rivet Small silver wire used to hold silver or material in place.

Rouge A polishing compound.

Saw frame A C-shape tool which holds a fine saw blade under tension between two ends.

Solder The metal material used to fuse metal together. Soldering is the process by which this is done.

Stake A steel form used to shape metal on.

Stretching In forging, the process by which metal is made longer or widened.

Tempering The condition resulting when silver is beaten and/or forged. It is the condition opposite to annealing.

Torch Any one of a number of devices—sizes, shapes, and fuels—employed to create and direct heat.

Vise A tool used to grip metal between parallel jaws.

A LIST OF BASIC TOOLS AND SUPPLIES

An asterisked (*) item is one that is nice to have but not absolutely necessary.

Cutting
Tin snips
Small snips (usually part of set with jeweler's pliers)*
Saw frame and blades (number 2 cut, number 2/0 cut, and number 4/0 cut), rough to fine

Filing (and holding)
Large "bastard" file (8 inches), flat (This can be a number 2 cut.)
Large half-round file
Large round file*
Needle files (6 inches)
   Flat, oval, and round (number 2 cut)
   Flat* (number 4 cut)
Bench pin (wooden clamp-on device for cutting)
Ring clamp
Pliers
   Flat
   Needle-nose
   Round
   (See above: small snips.)

Drilling
Small inexpensive hand drill
Bits (from ¼ inch to needle size—approximately six to ten)
Nail or ice pick

Bending
Rawhide mallet
Rubber mallet*
Wooden mallet*
Stakes or forms (mandrels, etc.)* (Use whatever is handy.)

Beating—forging, forming
Good (12- to 20-ounce) metal hammer with two faces, one slightly domed and the other very domed
Flat steel block, or reasonable alternative
Small rivet hammer*
12- to 16-ounce planishing hammer*
Lead block*

Annealing
Torch (Bernz O Matic) with small orifice
Charcoal block
Asbestos pad
Annealing pan* (Pumice in an old pot works fine.)

Soldering
Solder
   Easy
   Medium
   Hard
Hard silver solder flux and container (borax slate)
Sparex #2 (container)

Melting
(Same tools as used for soldering and annealing)

Setting stones
Findings
Gallery wire for bezels, stones

Finishing (polishing)
Emery cloth*
Crocus cloth
Pumice* (Ajax works almost as well.)
Polishing compounds
   Tripoli (At this stage, often use liver of sulfur; then . . .)
   Rouge

SOURCES OF SUPPLIES

Allcraft Tool and Supply Company, Inc.
100 Frank Rd.
Hicksville, N.Y. 11801
AND
204 North Harbor Blvd.
Fullerton, Calif. 92632

American Handicrafts
20 West 14th St.
New York, N.Y. 10011

Anchor Tool & Supply Company
12 John St.
New York, N.Y. 10038

ARE, Inc.
Box 155
North Montpelier Rd.
Plainfield, Vt. 05667

Craft Service
337 University Ave.
Rochester, N.Y. 14607

William Dixon Company
750 Washington Ave.
Carlstadt, N.J. 07072

Paul H. Gesswein & Company
235 Park Ave. South
New York, N.Y. 10003

Grieger's Inc.
1633 East Walnut St.
Pasadena, Calif. 91106

T. B. Hagstoz & Son
709 Sansom St.
Philadelphia, Pa. 19106

Kerr Manufacturing Company
6081 Twelfth St.
Detroit, Mich. 48174

C. & E. Marshall Company
Box 7737
Chicago, Ill. 60680

Marshall-Swartchild Company
2040 Milwaukee Ave.
Chicago, Ill. 60647

Metal Crafts Supply Company
10 Thomas St.
Providence, R.I. 02903

C. W. Somers & Company
387 Washington St.
Boston, Mass. 02124

Torit Manufacturing Company
1133 Rankin St.
St. Paul, Minn. 55116

BIBLIOGRAPHY

Bates, Kenneth F. *Enameling Principles and Practice.* Cleveland: The World Publishing Company, 1951. Revised 1972.

Baxter, William T. *Jewelry, Gem Cutting, and Metal Craft*, Revised Edition. New York: Whittlesey House, McGraw-Hill Book Company, Inc., 1942.

Bovin, Murray. *Casting.* Forest Hills, N.Y.: Murray Bovin, 1971.

Bovin, Murray. *Jewelry Making.* Forest Hills, N.Y.: Murray Bovin, 1952.

Brynner, Irena. *Jewelry: Design and Techniques.* New York: Reinhold Book Corporation, 1968.

Brynner, Irena. *Modern Jewelry.* New York: Van Nostrand Reinhold, 1968.

Choate, Sharr. *Creative Casting, Jewelry, Silverware, Sculpture.* New York: Crown Publishers, 1966.

Choate, Sharr. *Creative Gold and Silversmithing.* New York: Crown Publishers, 1972.

Cunynghame, H. H. *Art Enamelling on Metals.* London: A. Constable and Company, Inc., 1901.

Dipasquale, Dominic, Jean Delius, and Thomas Eckersley. *Jewelry Making*: *An Illustrated Guide to Technique.* Englewood Cliffs, N.J.: Prentice-Hall, Inc., 1975.

Evans, Joan. *A History of Jewellery, 1100–1870.* New York: Pitman Publishing Corporation, 1953.

Franke, Lois E. *Handwrought Jewelry.* Bloomington, Ill.: McKnight & McKnight Publishing Company, 1962.

Gentille, Thomas. *Step by Step Jewelry.* New York: Western Publishing Company, 1968.

Grando, Michael. *Jewelry Form and Technique.* Princeton, N.J.: Van Nostrand Reinhold, 1969.

Hughes, Graham. *Modern Jewelry.* New York: Crown Publishers, Inc., 1963.

Hughes, Graham. *Modern Silver.* New York: Crown Publishers, Inc., 1967.

Kronquist, Emil F. *Metalcraft and Jewelry.* Peoria, Ill.: The Charles A. Bennett Company, Inc., 1926.

Linick, Leslie. *Jeweler's Workshop Practices.* Chicago: Henry Paulson and Company, 1948.

Ludvig, Oswald A. *Metalwork: Technology and Practice.* Bloomington, Ill.: McKnight & McKnight Publishing Company, 1947.

Martin, Charles J. *How to Make Modern Jewelry.* New York: Museum of Modern Art, 1949.

Morton, Philip. *Contemporary Jewelry*: *A Studio Handbook.* New York: Holt, Reinhart and Winston, Inc., 1969.

Pack, Greta. *Jewelry and Enameling.* Princeton, N.J.: Van Nostrand Company, 1941.

Pack, Greta. *Jewelry Making for the Beginning Craftsman.* Princeton, N.J.: Van Nostrand Company, Inc., 1957.

Shoenfelt, Joseph. *Designing and Making Handwrought Jewelry.* New York: McGraw-Hill, 1960.

Sinkankas, A. *Gem Cutting*: *A Lapidary's Manual.* Princeton, N.J.: Van Nostrand Company, Inc., 1962.

Storey, Mickey. *Centrifugal Casting as a Jewelry Process.* Scranton, Pa.: International Textbook, 1963.

Thomas, Richard. *Metalsmithing for the Artist-Craftsman.* New York: Chilton Company, Book Division, 1960.

Untracht, Oppi. *Enameling on Metal.* Philadelphia: Chilton Company, 1957.

Untracht, Oppi. *Metal Techniques for Craftsmen.* Garden City, N.Y.: Doubleday and Company, 1968.

Von Neumann, Robert. *The Design and Creation of Jewelry.* New York: Chilton Company, Book Division, 1961. Revised Edition, 1972.

Wiener, Louis. *Handmade Jewelry.* Princeton, N.J.: Van Nostrand Company, Inc., 1948.

Willcox, Donald J. *New Design in Jewelry.* New York: Van Nostrand Company, 1970.

Winebrenner, D. Kenneth. *Jewelry Making as an Art Expression.* Scranton, Pa.: International Textbook Company, 1955.

Zarchy, Harry. *Jewelry-Making and Enameling.* New York: Alfred A. Knopf, Inc., 1959.